THE

FAERY
GUIDE

How connecting with
the Faery realms can bring
peace, love and happiness

Listen to your hearts,
follow your dreams
and let your light shine brightly.

For Faery Chlóe and Hobbit Tom

THE
FAERY
GUIDE

How connecting with
the Faery realms can bring
peace, love and happiness

Denise Whichello Brown

Published by SILVERDALE BOOKS
An imprint of Bookmart Ltd
Registered number 2372865
Trading as Bookmart Ltd
Desford Road
Enderby
Leicester LE19 4AD

2003 D&S Books Ltd

D&S Books Ltd
Kerswell,
Parkham Ash, Bideford
Devon, England
EX39 5PR

e-mail us at:-
enquiries@dsbooks.fsnet.co.uk

This edition printed 2003

ISBN 1-856057-38-0

Book Code DS0063 Faeries

Creative Director: Sarah King
Editor: Yvonne Worth
Project editor: Daniel Green
Photographer: Colin Bowling
Designer: Axis Design Editions

Fonts used in this book: Koch –
Antiqua, Arial and Helvetica.

Printed in China

1 3 5 7 9 10 8 6 4 2

CONTENTS

INTRODUCTION

Do you believe in Faeries?

I do and so does my daughter Chlóe and son Tom who have written the many beautiful poems that appear in this book!

We can assure you that Faeries (or nature spirits if you prefer!) most certainly DO exist. They are real and they are part of our world. Wherever there is nature they are to be found. Do not assume that just because you cannot see Faeries and because they cannot be scientifically proven they do not exist. The veil that separates us from the Faery realms is very thin — all you need to do is to let go of your doubts and the veil will lift. You may think that 'seeing is believing' but first you have to believe to see!

When I was first approached to write this book, I have to say that I was somewhat dubious (to say the least!) It is a fact that the majority of the population believe in angels – indeed I have written a highly successful book about them. But … Faeries … how many people believe in Faeries? A much smaller percentage of the population, I suggest – although more and more people are becoming convinced of their existence.

Then, I thought back to my childhood. How I loved to gaze for hours at pictures of the Faery realms. How fascinated I was as a little girl. What beautiful games I used to play with them and what wonderful friends they were. What a pity, I thought, that I was shamed into disbelief and disdain by my peers and by adults. People already think I'm peculiar because I work with the angels – I even run angel workshops would you believe? If I am already thought of as peculiar, then what have I got to lose! So I decided to take the plunge and open up my eyes to the wondrous world of Faeries. And I am pleased to tell you it is a very beautiful and inspiring world.

To my great surprise, just by 'thinking' about the Faery realms I began to draw close to me people who could actually see Faeries AND would admit to it! These individuals have helped me greatly on my voyage of discovery, as have my children, Chlóe and Tom, who have been a source of inspiration.

I began to realise why everyone who comes to the area in which I live calls it 'Faeryland'. I was amazed to find that the Faeries were right under my nose – my garden is absolutely teeming with nature spirits. I tried to 'sense' them and I was delighted to discover that I was able to feel their presence all around me – in the flowers, on the lawn and in the leaves and trees. It had never ever occurred to me before to look for the Faeries, but now I found I could almost see them in my mind's eye. They were not just fictitious creatures found in Faery tales, after all!

Whilst writing this book, I was guided to many places where Faeries can be found. I particularly enjoyed my visit to the enchanted forest of Brocéliande in Brittany, France where there is an abundance of nature spirits. I gazed upon Merlin's tomb and the Fountain of Barenton where Merlin met the Faery Vivien. I stared at the reflections in the clear water of the Faeries' Mirror and I revelled in the presence of the Faeries.

The purpose of this book is to share with you the nature of these radiant beings. I encourage you to acknowledge their existence, invite them into your daily life and co-operate and work with them. Let them touch your hearts and shape your dreams. Enjoy the magic of the Faeries!

Open up your eyes to the beauty of the Faery realms

Magic

Deep into the woods, where the soft river flows,
Lies the gap where the human world ends.
Where no more, the harsh wind blows
And then reality, becomes twisted and bends.

Faery whispers, hushed at first, stream into the night,
Touch you with hands that hold you tight.
They will never let you go,
Because they love you so,
This is Faery magic.

Dancing on the water, frolicking in the night sky,
The moon casts an eerie glow upon the world.
Fly mystical creatures, fly,
So all your magic can be unfurled
Illuminating the sky like tiny torch lights.

They take away your fears and fright;
You seem to understand
The dreams of the land
As your heart is convulsed by this Faery magic.

"Oh, I want to know so much about you" you cry,
How you brighten up the sky;
How you care for Mother Earth's creations;
How you possess our imaginations
With your Faery thoughts and desires;
How you burn our hate like fires.

But alas! It is morning.
They are gone
And all that remains
Is the babble of the brook
And the Faery whispers in your heart.

CHLÓE WHICHELLO

FAERIES IN
MYTH & LITERATURE

I know a bank where the wild thyme blows,
Where oxslips and the nodding violet grows,
Quite over-canopied with luscious woodbine,
With sweet musk-roses and with eglantine:
There sleeps Titania sometimes of the night,
Lull'd in these flowers with dances and delight,
And there the snake throws her enamell'd skin,
Weed wide enough to wrap a Fairy in,
And with the juice of this I'll streak her eyes,
And make her full of hateful fantasies.

OBERON

(EXCERPT FROM SHAKESPEARE'S 'A MIDSUMMER'S NIGHT DREAM', ACT 2, SCENE 1)

Faery stories, poems, ballads and songs have always fascinated and enchanted us and been passed down by word of mouth for hundreds of years. Faeries appear in literature at least as early as Homer's 'Iliad' and 'Odyssey' (c.850–800 BC), in which Faeries, nymphs and dryads are mentioned.

Where round the bed, whence Achelous springs,
That wat'ry dance in mazy rings.

('ILIAD', BOOK XXIV)

What sounds are those that gather from the shores,
The voice of nymphs that haunt the sylvan bowers,
The fair-hair'd dryads of the shady wood,
Or azure daughters of the silver flood?

('ODYSSEY', BOOK VI)

The earliest writing surviving in Britain dates from the 12th century. In 1188, Giraldus Cambrensis (Gerald de Barry), a distinguished writer, historian and ecclesiastic of the early Middle Ages, made a journey through Wales as he tried to gather support for the Third Crusade. He collected stories from the people he met on the way and detailed them in his chronicle, 'Itinerarium Cambriae'. One of the tales told to him by a priest who was adamant that it was his own experience, namely, 'Elidor and the Golden Ball', describes the experiences of a twelve-year-old boy in Faeryland. The Faeries were small, fair-haired, vegetarian, spoke a language similar to ancient Greek and had no wings. It is interesting how the appearance of Faeries has changed over the eight centuries since the first written description appeared. If you asked someone to describe a Faery nowadays most would say that Faeries do have wings. In the early chronicles however, Faeries were usually portrayed as having no wings. The butterfly-type wings were prevalent in Greek art where the soul or psyche was shown as a miniature human with wings.

In 1211, the medieval writer, Gervase of Tilbury, described small Faeries called 'Portunes'. These were totally different in appearance from those described by his contemporary Giraldus. They were half an inch (1.5 cm) in height, looked like wrinkled old men, wore ragged clothes and assisted agricultural workers. Portunes also carried frogs to roast on farmhouse fires!

Walter Map, Archdeacon of Oxford and another 12th-century chronicler, tells the story of Wild Edric in 'De Nugis Curialium' in which he describes Faeries as being taller than humans!

An early ballad, 'Thomas the Rhymer', written anonymously, relates the story of Thomas of Earlston, a 13th-century poet who was visited by the Queen of Elfland as he lay under a magical elder tree on Huntlie Bank in Scotland. In return for a kiss, he agreed to go to Faeryland with her and remain there for seven years. As a reward, the Queen bestowed upon him the gifts of prophecy, poetry and a magical harp. Thomas describes the beautiful Queen:

Her skirt was of the grass-green silk,
Her mantel of the velvet fine,
At ilka tett of her horse's mane,
Hung fifty silver bells and nine.

True Thomas he took off his hat,
And bowed him low down till his knee:
"All hail, thou mighty Queen of Heaven!
For your peer on earth I never did see."

"O no, O no, True Thomas," she says,
"That name does not belong to me;
I am but the queen of fair Elfland,
And I'm come here for to visit thee."

The famous Chaucer mentions Faeries in 'The Canterbury Tales' on several occasions. He spoke of a land filled with Faeries, in the opening of 'The Wyf of Bath's Tale':

In th'olde dayes of the Kyng Arthour,
Of which that Britons speken greet honour,
Al was this land fulfild of fayerye.
The elf-queene, with hir joly compaignye,
Daunced ful ofte in many a grene mede.
This was the olde opinion, as I rede;
I speke of manye hundred yeres ago.
But now kan no man se none elves mo,

King Arthur, who was a major figure in Faery literature, was associated with Faeries such as the infamous Morgan the Fey and Vivien, Lady of the Lake, who bewitched Merlin the magician. In 1485, came the publication of 'Le Morte D'Arthur', written by Sir Thomas Mallory. In 1534, the 'Huon of Bordeaux' was translated by Lord Berners. King Arthur, Morgan le Fey and Oberon, the most famous of all the Faery kings, appear in this book. In the tale, Oberon presents Huon with his bride, Escleremand, and proclaims him to be heir to Faeryland. 'Huon of Bordeaux' is a highly influential piece of literature that was used by Shakespeare as his source for his famous 'A Midsummer Night's Dream', written c.1594. The Arthurian legend is discussed in more detail later in this chapter.

Faeries appear in many of Shakespeare's plays. In 'Romeo and Juliet', written in 1595, Mab, the Faeries' midwife, is described by Mercutio:

O, then, I see Queen Mab hath been with you.
She is the fairies' midwife, and she comes
In shape no bigger than an agate-stone
On the fore-finger of an alderman

Mercutio describes Queen Mab as a small, delicate insect who rides around on a hazelnut:

Her waggon-spokes made of long spinners' legs,
The cover of the wings of grasshoppers …
Her waggoner a small grey-coated gnat …
Her chariot is an empty hazel-nut
Made by the joiner squirrel or old grub …

In 'A Midsummer Night's Dream', the Faeries are portrayed as tiny little beings – in contrast to Titania, Queen of the Faeries, who is mortal size. The Faeries and elves attend to the whims of Oberon the King and Titania the Queen. The mischievous, shapeshifter Puck is their chief messenger. He pretends to be a three-legged stool and a crab apple in a bowl of punch. A Faery says of the exploits of Puck:

… are not you he
That frights the maidens of the villagery;
Skim milk, and sometimes labour in the quern
And bootless make the breathless housewife churn …
Mislead night-wanderers, laughing at their harm?
Those that Hobgoblin call you and sweet Puck,
You do their work, and they shall have good luck:
Are not you he?

('A Midsummer Night's Dream', Act 2, Scene 1)

The last of Shakespeare's plays to incorporate Faeries is 'The Tempest' written around 1611. Ariel can create tempests, take on any form and also become invisible. During the 16th and 17th centuries a great deal of literature was inspired by Faeries. An example of this is Ben Johnson's masque (a dance drama with verse commentary), 'Oberon, the Fairy Prince', performed in 1611. It was designed to honour Henry, Prince of Wales, who, aged 16, took the title role.

It was dangerous, however, to believe in Faeries at this time. Witch-hunts were taking place and anyone who confessed to seeing Faeries was liable to be burned as a witch.

By the 18th century, poets were mostly uninterested in Faeries. The poet and painter William Blake was an exception. He believed a Faery funeral had taken place in his back garden. He described the Faeries he had seen to be the size of a grasshopper.

At the time of the witch—hunts, belief in Faeries could be dangerous.

The early 18th century saw the introduction of the idea of Faery Godmothers. Faery stories were now regarded as suitable reading material for children, since they taught them human morals.

In the 19th century there was a great desire to seek and find an explanation for the belief in Faeries. Many theories were put forward. The most common theory saw Faeries as souls of the dead and Faeryland as the place where souls await the Last Judgment. Another theory, which was particularly popular in Ireland, saw Faeries as fallen angels who wandered the earth, as they were not allowed to enter neither Heaven nor Hell.

In 1823, the first English edition of German Popular Stories by the German brothers Grimm was published. By 1850, the Faerytales of Hans Christian Andersen were being translated into several different languages.

In the early 20th century came one of the best-known Faery stories, 'Peter Pan'. It was originally known as 'The Little White Bird' when Sir James Matthew Barrie wrote it in 1902. Most of us are very familiar with the boy who never grew up but stayed in Never Never Land with Tinkerbell the Faery.

The 20th century has seen the publication of the classic works of Professor Tolkien, 'The Hobbit' and 'The Lord of the Rings'. The characters include elves, goblins, dwarfs, orcs, hobbits and the wizard Gandalf. Tolkien's books fascinate adults possibly more than children. Lord of the Rings is now a blockbuster movie.

> Three Rings for the Elven-kings under the sky,
> Seven for the Dwarf-lords in their halls of stone,
> Nine for Mortal Men doomed to die,
> One for the Dark Lord on his dark throne
> In the Land of Mordor where the Shadows lie.
> One Ring to rule them all, One Ring to find them,
> One Ring to bring them all and in the darkness bind them
> In the Land of Mordor where the Shadows lie.

In the 21st century, it looks like our fascination for stories of magic and enchantment is here to stay. They will continue to capture the imagination of writers.

Faeries have also, of course, been an inspiration for many painters. 'A Midsummer Night's Dream' inspired many artists. The Faery illustrations of Mabel Lucie Attwell and Cicely Mary Barker have delighted both adults and children alike. Our belief in them still persists.

The Mystery of the Cottingley Faeries – FACT or FICTION?

The most famous documented sighting of Faeries took place at the beginning of this century. In July 1917, two young girls, Elsie Wright, aged 15, and her cousin Frances Griffiths, aged 11, produced some photographs of Faeries. Elsie lived with her parents in Cottingley, England and her cousin was staying with her family for the summer holidays. Elsie told Frances about the Faeries in the woods that she often played with and during the holidays, the girls borrowed Elsie's father's camera and took pictures. One picture showed Frances with five tiny, winged Faeries dancing around her and the other was of Frances in conversation with a gnome.

Elsie's father was very sceptical about the photographs. However, in May 1920, the pictures were shown to Mr. Edward L. Gardener, a well-known figure in the Theosophical Movement. A photographic expert, Mr. Harold Snelling, examined the photographs. He pronounced them to be untouched single exposures and pointed out that the wings of the creatures were moving at the time of the exposure! How could 'fake' figures have moved whilst they were being photographed? Experts at Kodak, however, were rather doubtful about the authenticity of the photographs.

Mr. Gardener took the pictures to the eminent Sir Arthur Conan Doyle who was convinced that they were absolutely genuine. He wrote an article about the pictures in the Strand Magazine and in his book published in 1922, 'The Coming of the Fairies'. Gardener returned to Cottingley and asked the girls to take more Faery pictures under controlled conditions. The girls produced three more Faery photographs.

These photographs really captured the imagination of the public. Many believed them to be real. No one has ever really produced a watertight explanation for the Faery pictures. Some have suggested that the Faeries were really paper cut-outs made to stand up with hat pins – Elsie was quite an accomplished artist and the watercolour Faeries which she drew were very similar to those photographed. The Cottingley Faeries still remain a mystery. Warner Bros. Made this story into a captivating film, 'Fairy Tale, A True Story', in 1997, which is a delight to see.

FAERIES AND ARTHURIAN LEGEND

Probably the most famous legend connected with the Faery world is that of King Arthur. There are many conflicting opinions as to whether there was a real king Arthur, and the legend itself has many versions — although they all have in common a strong link with the Faery realms. Here I've concentrated on the most widely known version of the Arthurian myth.

Arthurian legend has its origins in Celtic mythology. Later stories from French and British writers embellished the myth, creating an exciting and romantic tale that has fascinated and entertained us throughout the ages. Even today, King Arthur is an inspiration for many films, novels and poems. The southwest of England and Brocéliande, the enchanted forest of Brittany, are especially renowned as settings for one of the most enduring myths in western mythology. In this chapter we will look at some of the Faery beings found in the Arthurian legends along with places to reflect on this enchanted world.

KING ARTHUR

King Arthur has many associations with the Faery realm, in particular Merlin, Morgan le Fey (Arthur's half-sister), Vivian (the Lady of the Lake) and Guinevere.

Arthur is said to have been born at Tintagel as a result of magic and subterfuge. The date of his birth is unclear but is believed to have been around 480–500 AD. According to legend, Uther Pendragon, King of the Britains, fell hopelessly in love with the beautiful Lady Igraine (Ygraine, Ygerna) wife of Gorlois, the Duke of Tintagel. She is said to have been of Faery blood. When the Duke heard of the King's love he immediately took her away to his impregnable castle at Tintagel, whereupon Uther enlisted the help of Merlin, the magician. Merlin agreed to help the King on the condition that Uther give into his keeping the son that would be conceived by Igraine the first time

One of the stories of Excalibur suggests it was given to Arthur by the mysterious lady of the lake.

they made love. Uther agreed and Merlin used his secret powers to make the King look like Gorlois himself. Igraine received him with grace since she believed he was her husband. When the child was born Uther kept his promise, and Merlin took the baby to the nobleman, Sir Ector (alias Cynyr Ceinfarfog, the Fair Bearded). Ector and his wife named the child Arthur, and brought him up as a brother to their own son, Sir Kay. Ector and his family remained unaware as to the true identity of the young boy.

The events of the famous 'sword in the stone' legend occurred about 16 years later when Ector and his retinue travelled to a great tournament. Close to the location of the tournament was a great stone, bearing the inscription, 'Whoever can pull this sword out of this stone will be King of England.' Many had tried to remove the sword, but none had succeeded. Realising that Sir Kay had forgotten his sword, Ector sent Arthur back to retrieve it. On the way back, Arthur saw the sword in the stone, and decided taking it would be quicker than fetching Sir Kay's own sword. Not knowing the legend attached to the sword, Arthur withdrew it easily and took it to Sir Kay. Sir Kay recognised it to be the sword in the stone and told Sir Ector that as he had the famous sword, he should surely be the true king. Eventually, however, Sir Kay's feelings of guilt led him to confess to Sir Ector what had really happened – that it had really been Arthur who pulled the sword out. At first nobody believed him. So the sword was returned to the stone and Arthur was challenged to remove it once more. He succeeded, and was acclaimed as King of England. According to another legend, Arthur was given the sword, Excalibur, at a later date, by the Lady of the Lake.

As a man, Arthur fell in love and became betrothed to Guinevere, daughter of King Leodegrance, who may have been of Faery origin. They were married after Arthur's great victory on Salisbury Plain where Arthur was confirmed as King of 'les deux Bretagnes' (Great Britain and Brittany). In later stories, Guinevere's dowry was the round table – around which Arthur based his court, and founded the famous Knights of the Round Table. There are many tales of the hero-knights searching for the life-renewing Holy Grail that had held the sacred blood from the Cross.

Arthur won many famous battles driving the Saxons out of Great Britain and Brittany. His most famous victory was at The Battle of Mount Baden, 516 AD, the last of his twelve great battles. As a result, peace was restored to the Wessex Area of England for fifty years.

Unfortunately Arthur was not so lucky in love. He had a son, Mordred, conceived either by Morgan le Fey herself, or another of his half-sisters, having been tricked to her bed by Morgan's enchantment. His beloved wife, Guinevere betrayed him with Sir Lancelot, one of his knights, and it was Mordred who discovered Guinevere and Lancelot and brought the news to his father. Arthur was forced to condemn Guinevere to death, but she was saved by Sir Lancelot at the last minute.

Arthur travelled to France to fight Lancelot, leaving his son, Mordred, as regent. In Arthur's absence, Mordred proclaimed his father dead and took the throne for himself. Arthur and Mordred eventually met at the Battle of Camlann, which took place around 537 AD. When the battle ended, only Mordred, Arthur and Sir Bedivere remained. Arthur and Mordred fought to the death, leaving Arthur the victor, but fatally wounded. At Arthur's request, Sir Bedivere threw the sword, Excalibur, back into the lake. After his death, Arthur was taken by Faeries to Avalon, an island in a lake, to be healed. Some believe that Avalon is near Île Aval, just off the coast of northern Brittany; others say the Isle of Avalon is at Glastonbury. It was after the supposed discovery of Arthur's grave in 1911 that Glastonbury became known as Avalon.

In Tennyson's poem 'The Idylls of the King', the mortally wounded Arthur departs:

> To the island-valley of Avilion;
> Where falls not hail, or rain, or any snow,
> Nor ever wind blows loudly; but it lies
> Deep-meadowed, happy, fair with orchard lawns
> And bowery hollows crowned with summer sea,
> Where I will heal me of my grievous wound.'

Legend has it that the Faeries have guarded him ever since in a mysterious sleep, where he will remain until he is needed.

MORGAN LE FEY

Morgan the Faery, also known as Morgana le Fey, or Morgen, is one of the most famous of all Faery queens (le Fey means 'of the Faeries' in French). She is often described as the half-sister of King Arthur, well-versed in magic that she learnt from Merlin. She is knowledgeable in many subjects, including medicine and astronomy. This enchantress understands the properties of all plants and uses them for her magic and healing. She is skilled in the art of shapeshifting and is able to transform into any bird or animal of her choosing.

Morgan is a woman of great beauty, tall with long, shiny black hair that she sometimes plaits. Her face may be playful and cheerful, dreamy and enchanted, betrayed and disillusioned or angry and resentful. She often dresses in robes of green.

Although Morgan has inhabited Tintagel and Camelot, her real homes are Avalon and the 'Valley of No Return' where she can still be found today. Morgan spent the early part of her life in Tintagel and visited the Isle of Avalon where she soon became Queen. After the death of her stepfather, Uther Pendragon, she went to Camelot, where Arthur and Guinevere resided. Guinevere's cousin, the handsome knight Guyomar, visited the castle one day and they fell deeply in love with each other. They met in secret but were one day discovered by Guinevere, who forbade them ever to see each other again. Morgan was furious with her and despised Guinevere for the rest of her life.

Morgan was full of sorrow, but she was to suffer yet another blow that would turn her into a Faery of vengeance. She fell in love with a Knight but was betrayed by him. The Knight and his lover arranged to meet in a beautiful green valley. Morgan caught them and wreaked her revenge by turning them into stone and putting a spell on the valley. Faithful lovers may cross without risk, but anyone guilty of the slightest unfaithfulness, whether in thought or deed, is forced to stay there, imprisoned by an invisible force.

This valley of the unfaithful is found in Brocéliande in Brittany, France. It is known as the 'Val Sans Retour' (the Valley of No Return) or the 'Val des Faux-Amants' (Valley of Faithless Lovers). I have visited this beautiful place, which is a maze of valleys. The 'Rock of the Faux Amants' dominates the valley and as you walk through it you seem to lose all notion of time.

Eighteen years later, Lancelot passed through the valley. Morgan could not imprison him, since he was faithful to Guinevere. She tried to defeat him but he was not afraid of her magic. Lancelot broke the enchantment and Morgan had to give up her prisoners.

Morgan le Fey was furious and put a curse on Arthur and his Kingdom. However, following Arthur's final battle with the treacherous Mordred, Morgan was one of the Faeries who transported him to the Isle of Avalon.

To enter the Val Sans Retour you pass the beautiful 'Miroir aux Fées' (Faeries' Mirror). You become aware that there is a completely different world beyond the mirror. You pass through the doorway to the world of Faery enchantment and legends.

THE FAERY VIVIEN – LADY OF THE LAKE

Various names are given to the Lady of the Lake, including Vivien, Vivienne, Nineve, Nimue and Niniane.

Vivien's lake is usually thought to be in Brocéliande in Brittany, France, but some say she lives in Dosmary Pool on Bodmin Moor in Cornwall. Her father, Diones or Dinas, a 'vavasour' (holder of feudal lands), who served the Duke of Bourgogne, was said to have been the goddess Diana's godchild. This is why Vivien is, herself, sometimes depicted as Diana the Huntress. Usually, however, she is drawn with long wavy hair that forms an aura around her whole body. Vivien is slender and youthful with a delicate mouth, an upturned nose and pink cheeks. Her eyes are large and enchanting. The Lady of the Lake has a captivating charm.

Vivien first encountered Merlin at the Fountain of Barenton deep in the forest of Brocéliande. Although, since Merlin could see into the fountain, he was aware of the trap that Vivien would one day weave, he found that he could not hold back from the desires that filled his mind. The youthful, beautiful Vivien had always lived in this forest. Her father lived in Comper Castle in Brocéliande. She spent many days with the other Faeries of the forest as they admired their reflection in the water of the 'Faeries' Mirror'. When Vivien met Merlin, at the age of fifteen, she was fascinated by his power and knowledge. They sat at the edge of the fountain talking endlessly. Merlin was utterly charmed by her and did not leave Barenton until she had promised to love him in exchange for his knowledge and magical powers.

Every day Merlin taught Vivien new magical spells. He also taught her the antidotes of magic against magic and even taught her spells that can never be broken. At Comper Castle, Merlin created a castle for her in the nearby lake to please her. He built this crystal palace for her in just one night. Merlin made the castle invisible to others so that no one would ever bother her. All others would see would be the water of a lake. Vivien was delighted and from then on called herself 'Lady of the Lake'.

Yet, the Faery Vivien wished to know even more. Her wish was to learn all Merlin's secrets and then imprison him so that she could keep him close to her forever. She persuaded him to teach her a spell of imprisonment. A little later when Merlin fell asleep on the grass, Vivien drew a magic circle around him that imprisoned him in an invisible palace.

At first Arthur was not concerned about Merlin's disappearance, but when he had still not returned a year later, Arthur sent Gauvin to search Brittany for him. As Gauvin rode through the forest of Brocéliande he heard the voice of Merlin through the invisible walls that separated him from the visible world. Merlin told Gauvin to tell Arthur that he would never see him again.

Vivien first encountered Merlin at the Barenton Fountain, deep in the forest of Brocéliande, in Brittany

Vivien is not only renowned for being the Faery who imprisoned Merlin, but also as the foster mother of Sir Lancelot, famous Knight of the Round Table. In some versions Vivien is said to have found the orphaned baby Lancelot at the edge of the lake, while in another she snatches him from his mother Queen Helen. Vivien took Lancelot down to the bottom of the lake and raised him as her own child. She prepared him for his greatness by teaching him the arts of weaponry. When he was fifteen Vivien told him that it was time for him to leave and become a Knight of the Round Table. Lancelot, extremely handsome, dressed all in white showed himself to be the best of Knights. His downfall was to fall in love with King Arthur's wife, Guinevere.

In some legends, the enchantress Vivien is also thought to have given Arthur his magic sword Excalibur. Merlin took Arthur to the lake of clear water and a sleeve of white silk holding a sword by its scabbard (blade protector) appeared. The scabbard was magical — when carrying the scabbard no harm could befall Arthur, no matter how deep his wounds were, he would not bleed.

Vivien can still be found in the Forest of Brocéliande. Look for her around the Fountain of Barenton and try to catch a glimpse of her at the bottom of the pond of Comper Castle.

However, take care as you venture deep into the woods close to the Fountain of Barenton or any other springs in the forest. You could encounter a Corrigan, otherwise known as a Corriganed, Corrikét or a Korrigan. Corrigans are female Faeries who guard sacred springs and fountains of Brittany — although you may also encounter them in Cornwall.

At night-time Corrigans seduce men by appearing as beautiful blonde maidens. If a man beholds a naked Corrigan bathing in the springs he must marry her within three days or die. At first light Corrigans appear as repulsive hags. Men who see a Corrigan at night find it impossible to forget her. However, it is said that if a man genuinely loves her in both her beautiful and her ugly forms she can become human and remain beautiful by day as well as by night. Corrigans are shapeshifters and can turn into spiders or snakes. If they see pretty children they will steal them and replace them with Faery changelings.

MERLIN

Merlin or Myrddin is a magician, wise man, counsellor and prophet and is a key figure in the legends of King Arthur. Many books, plays and films have been entirely devoted to Merlin and he has re-emerged in other guises, such as Gandalf in J.R.R. Tolkien's 'The Lord of the Rings'.

Merlin, the magician, was half-Faery. He was the illegitimate son of a monastic Royal Princess of Dyfed. Some say his father was an angel, whereas others say his father was an incubus, an evil spirit that ravished his mother in her sleep. Merlin was endowed with great powers and he could speak as soon as he was born. When he was baptised as a child the evil apparently left Merlin, but fortunately his magical powers remained intact. He was given the name Emrys (or Ambrosius) at his birth in Carmarthen. He only later became known as Merlin, a Latinised version of the Welsh word, Myrddin, taken from the place of his birth.

In Great Britain, when King Constantine died he left two children, Constans (in French tales he is called 'Moine', but this word merely signifies a monk) and Uther Pendragon. When Constans was made King, Vortigern bribed some men to burst into Constans' sleeping chamber and cut off his head. Vortigern then became King. Vortigern tried to build a fortified tower in the mountains of Snowdonia in Wales. However, the tower kept collapsing. His astrologers and scholars told him that the tower would stay up if a seven-year-old, fatherless child were sacrificed. Two of his soldiers found Merlin who was able to save himself from sacrifice by explaining why the tower would not stand up. He said that two dragons, one red and one white, lived under the tower. Vortigern ordered the site to be dug and the two dragons emerged and began to fight. According to Merlin the red dragon was the Britains and the white dragon the Saxons. This meant that Vortigern would be slain and Ambrosius Aurelianus, then Uther Pendragon and then Arthur would take the throne. Merlin's prophecy came true and established Merlin as a prophet. Merlin was asked to stay at court and although Merlin declined the offer, he promised to help the King.

Ambrosius summoned Merlin to ask him to think of a suitable memorial for 460 British Kings and warriors who had been massacred by the Saxons. Merlin, together with Ambrosius' brother, Uther went to Ireland to procure the stones of the Giant's Ring from Mount Killaraus in Ireland. By his magic powers, Merlin brought them back and erected them near Amesbury – the place we now call Stonehenge. Geoffrey of Monmouth, a Welsh cleric who later became Bishop of St. Asaph, tells us this story in 1135, in his 'History of the Kings of Britain'.

When Ambrosius died he was succeeded by Uther Pendragon. Merlin magically disguised him to appear like Gorlois, the Duke of Tintagel so that the Duke's wife Lady Igraine (Ygraine, Ygerna) would allow him into her bed. Arthur was conceived and Merlin acted as Arthur's mentor and counsellor until he, Merlin, was imprisoned by the Faery Vivien (see pages 22–23). Perhaps if Merlin had not been imprisoned Arthur would have not been killed at the Battle of Camlann.

There is much speculation as to where Merlin's prison and/or burial place is to be found. Suggestions are 'Le Tombeau de Merlin' (Merlin's Tomb) near Paimpont in the legendary Forest of Brocéliande, France, beneath Merlin's Mound at Marlborough College in Marlborough (Wiltshire), at Drumelzier in Tweeddale (Scotland) and at Bryn Myrddin (Merlin's Hill) near Carmarthen (Wales).

I have visited Merlin's tomb in the Forest of Brocéliande. It is a very simple affair but a very special place, as it has been a place of worship for many centuries. The trees around it are decorated with wild flowers, ribbons and messages with wishes written on them. They are sacred Faery trees – the oak, holly and the hawthorn. The energy of Merlin is very much alive in this forest. It is a joyful, revitalising energy of contentment.

I have also visited Merlin's Mound in the grounds of Marlborough College. It is the second biggest man-made hill after the famous Silbury Hill five miles away at Avebury. Interestingly, I climbed to the top of the mound with no problems but on my way down, having decided to take a circular route, felt stuck and was unable to move for a few minutes. At the time I did not know of the imprisonment of Merlin but 'imprisoned' was exactly how I felt. As I drove away from the mound a double rainbow appeared – symbol of hope and perhaps a sign that Merlin's magic is still around.

Merlin's Tomb in the forest of Brocéliande

WHAT ARE FAERIES?

The word 'Faery' is most probably derived from the Latin word 'fatae' meaning the Fates or 'fatum' meaning destiny or enchantment. An early meaning of 'Faery' was 'Fay-erie', which referred to a state of enchantment. But then it changed in meaning to signify the beings who are responsible for the state of enchantment.

It is my belief that everything in nature such as flowers, trees, forests, wells, streams, rivers, lakes, mountains, crystals and so forth is endowed, guided and protected by a spirit. The function of angels is to guard, protect and help to heal us — whereas Faeries are the guardians and protectors of nature — they magnify the beauty that exists all around us. Faeries help us feel euphoric, playful and full of love and joy.

THE CLASSIFICATION OF FAERIES

Many attempts have been made to divide the Faery realm into categories. For example, in one popular system of classification, Faeries are divided into four main groups which are based on the elements:

Air (e.g. all winged Faeries, sylphs)

Earth (e.g. gnomes, brownies)

Water (e.g. undines, nixies, lamias)

Fire (e.g. salamanders, fire drakes)

According to Eastern philosophy there are Golden Devas, White Devas, Green Devas and Violet Devas. The Irish divide their Faeries into gnomes, leprechauns, Little People and the Sidhe. Others divide Faeries into Trooping Faeries and Solitary Faeries.

To classify Faeries is a difficult task, but, for the purpose of this book, I have classified the Faeries according to where they can be found – Faeries of the flowers, forests, trees, lakes streams etc. The location in which they are found will determine the shape and form that Faeries take and also their function.

WHAT DO FAERIES LOOK LIKE?

Faeries are pure energy – gentle, ethereal, exquisite creatures of light that can appear in many different forms. In fact, the form they adopt is changeable and is responsive to our thoughts and emotions. Faeries are a reflection of the inner nature of our souls. The form they present is dependent upon the mind of the person who is looking at them. Faeries are capable of taking whatever shape we want them to. One person may see Faeries as specks or beams of radiant light, whereas another may see them with wings.

FAERY SIZE

Faeries come in many different shapes and sizes. Some are so tiny they look like specks of dust as they dance around, whereas others can be huge such as the Faery forms that guard ancient sites.

FAERY BODIES

Their bodies are usually wispy, ethereal and translucent and can be a variety of the most beautiful 'out-of-this-world' colours. Some Faeries, such as the stone Faeries, are denser and much more solid. Other Faeries have hideous, distorted, grotesquely misshapen bodies. Some are expert shapeshifters and can transform into animals such as birds or snakes or may appear as beautiful women by night and repulsive hags by day.

FAERY WINGS

Their wings (if they possess them!) are similar to those of butterflies or dragonflies.

FAERY EARS

Faery ears are slightly rounded at the bottom yet very pointed at the top. In fact, they resemble the shape of Faery wings.

FAERY EYES

Faery eyes are the windows of the soul. Their eyes are deep and full of wisdom.

WHERE TO FIND FAERIES

Faeries can be found all over the world – they are not confined to particular places. They may be found in any landscape in every flower, bush and tree, in every brook, river and stream, well and spring, at the ocean's edge, in woods and forests, on every hill and mountain and around every stone and ancient site.

The magical Faery spirits are particularly attracted to everything green and to all forms of water since their purpose is to act as guardians of nature. They do prefer a wild natural setting rather than an artificial garden. You are least likely to find them in busy crowded towns and cities. Faeries are not easily found in shops, offices and supermarkets! They are repelled and affected by environmental pollution and pesticides, for Faeries are the protectors of Planet Earth.

Seeking Faeries

If seeking the Faeries is what you desire look in the
greenest and lushest of places.
Not in a supermarket or under a tyre or stooping
down to tie your laces!
Hide and go seek
Until their little faces will peep;
The Faeries are waiting for you to find
And leave you thinking you've lost your mind.
Near a stream, a river or tree,
Look in these places to seek Faery
Or wake up a deeper quest, look in your heart.
Commune with the Faeries, why don't you start?

CHLOE WHICHELLO

A Faery Ring.

FAERY RINGS

Perfect circles in the grass, commonly known as 'Faery rings', can often be seen. According to folklore these rings are created by Faeries dancing in the grass in the moonlight. Air photos show Faery rings as large as 200 yards (200 m) in diameter. Such large rings are thought to be more than 600 years old. Even nowadays it is considered to be wise to keep out of them. It is thought that some misfortune will befall anyone who steps into a Faery ring.

Many folk tales and songs tell of mortals who have been lured into Faery rings by the sound of Faery music. Once inside there is no escape. One is forced to dance without stopping until dawn, for years or sometimes forever! An evening spent dancing in a Faery ring is many years in the human realm, and mortals enticed into Faery rings find, on returning home, that many years have passed and their families are long gone. It is even dangerous to jump inside an empty Faery ring, for you will die at a young age. However, as long as you stay outside the ring you will not be enchanted. If you wish to see Faeries, run nine times clockwise round the outside of a Faery ring. Toadstools are often associated with Faeries, as shown by several of their names such as Yellow Fairy Club, Slender Elf Cap and Dune Pixiehood.

If You See A Faery Ring

If you see a Faery ring
In a field of grass,
Very lightly step around,
Tip-toe as you pass.
Last night Faeries frolicked there
And they're sleeping somewhere near.
If you see a tiny Faery
Lying fast asleep,
Shut your eyes
And run away,
Do not stay to peek!
Do not tell
Or you'll break a Faery spell.

AUTHOR UNKNOWN

CONNECTING WITH THE
FAERY REALMS

All of us can learn to see the normally invisible Faery world which exists all around us. At the moment you may perceive an empty forest but, one day soon with the help of this book, you may be able to see Faeries dancing around in a ring!

1 Start by going out into your own garden. If you do not have a garden then try to venture into any area of natural beauty where there are flowers and trees. Choose a time when it is very quiet and you can sit for a few moments on your own. Early in the morning is an excellent time, as is dusk, especially if the moon is full. Always take a notepad and pen with you to record any Faery experiences.

2 Begin to converse quietly with the nature spirits. Hold the intention that you wish to connect with the Faeries. Tell them either silently or verbally how much you wish to communicate with them. Faeries are highly sensitive beings who delight in attention. The more attention you give them the more likely they are to reveal themselves to you.

3 Start to examine all the different plants that surround you. Gently stroke and caress the leaves and inhale the fragrance of the flowers.

4 Be guided by the Faeries as to where you should sit. Make sure that you are comfortable and relaxed. Personally, I love to sit cross-legged but choose whichever position you wish.

5 Feel yourself strongly connected with the earth. It is helpful to imagine roots extending deep down into the centre of the earth establishing a strong connection.

6 Become aware of your breathing and, as you exhale, feel all the tension leaving your body. Feel it being released all the way down into the centre of the earth. You may find that you sigh deeply as the tension is dissolved.

7 As you become relaxed and calm begin to repeat silently or aloud an affirmation such as:
· I am sensitive and open to the Faery realms.
· I wish to communicate with the nature spirits.
· I wish to work with the spirits of nature.
By repeating one of these affirmations (or one of your own) your mind will empty itself of its mental baggage. Any thoughts going round and round in your head will begin to subside.

8 When you feel totally relaxed let your attention start to drift. Notice any sensations that you may feel. Accept any impressions you receive without questioning them. Do not have any expectations about what you might see, hear or feel. If you try too hard you will block yourself to receiving any communication.

9 Ask the Faeries to reveal themselves to you. Tell them that you wish to see them. Some people are able to see Faeries with their eyes closed, whereas others prefer to gently soften their focus and gaze.

10 Stay in the presence of the Faery realms for as long as you wish. You may be filled with an overwhelming sense of love and peace. Your eyes may even fill with tears in response to the beauty of the Faery world.

11 When you feel ready to return become very aware of the grass or the ground beneath you. Gently wiggle your fingers and toes.

12 Record any Faery experiences immediately afterwards in your Faery notebook. You may wish to do this in the form of words, symbols or even as a simple drawing if you are artistically inclined.

Try to repeat this exercise as often as you can. Be patient with yourself – just because you do not receive a Faery impression the first time does not mean that you never will! It may take you several attempts before you experience anything. But don't give up! The Faeries will reveal themselves to you eventually. I would be very surprised if you were unable to see or feel nothing after a week or two. The more the Faeries feel loved and appreciated the more they will pour into your garden!

FAERY SIGNS

The Faery realms will try to communicate their presence to you in many different ways:

You may notice sparkling, twinkly specks of light dancing around you. You may see them jumping from flower to flower or circling round the plants. As your vision improves you may start to see the spirits of the Faery world in greater detail. You may be able to detect wings, bodies and even faces.

You may feel the presence of the Faeries around you. The fluttering of their wings can feel like a gentle breeze or a rush of cold air. It is a common experience to feel a tickling sensation as they brush past you. Often your nose will start to tingle!

You may notice a petal or a leaf on your lap at the end of your exercise. This is a gift from the Faeries and a sure sign that they are around and waiting to communicate with you.

You may hear the Faeries communicating with you. It is common to hear Faery giggles as the Faery folk delight and revel in the idea that you love and appreciate them.

You may become aware of the most exquisite fragrance around you. This aroma may or may not be familiar to you. Every Faery has its own particular fragrance that can depend upon the function of that individual Faery! — imagine the beautiful perfume of a nature spirit who protects and cares for a jasmine plant or a rose bush!

You may experience a sense of love and peace as the Faery Kingdom embraces you and opens up your heart. You may even burst into laughter!

Whatever your experiences may be, enjoy connecting with the Faery Kingdom.

CREATING A FAERY SPACE IN YOUR HOUSE

You may like to create a special Faery space in your home to produce a focal point for drawing the nature spirits close to you. It is so easy to do!

Cover a small table or even part of a window sill with a piece of fabric — silk is particularly suitable since the Faery folk are attracted to natural fabrics.

Place a small statue on the Faery table that expresses how a Faery looks to you. These are readily available particularly now that the popularity of Faeries is growing so rapidly. You can also buy Faery dolls — I have 'Dizzy Daisy Fairweather' on one of my mantelpieces sitting on top of a crystal!

If you wish to attract the flower Faeries place a flower, leaf or a plant pot on your Faery table.

If you sense the nature spirits of the trees, place a small branch, twig, leaf or fruit on your Faery table.

A stone that you may have collected from a sacred site or any place that is special to you may also be added.

If you wish to sense the crystal Faeries then place some of your favourite pieces on your table.

Place a small bowl of water onto your Faery table, sprinkle a few drops of essential oil into it. Use whichever aromas appeal to you. The floral essential oils such as camomile, geranium, rose, jasmine, neroli and ylang ylang are particularly suitable.

This book, or any special Faery picture, may also be placed on your Faery table.

It is entirely up to you what you choose to put in your Faery space. The very action of creating it shows the Faery realms that you are reaching out and wish to commune with them, building a bridge between the two worlds. If you reach out to the nature spirits they will co-operate and answer you.

Try to spend a few moments sitting quietly in your Faery space and tune into to the Faeries that you are inviting to connect with you. You may find it helpful to pick up and hold your crystal(s) or stones. You may want to ripple the water with your hand or enjoy the fragrance of the flowers.

Contemplate the response you receive. Always give thanks to the elementals who have joined you. Make sure that you always write down any impressions. In time the energy will accumulate, making it easier for you to commune with the Faeries.

FAERIES
OF THE FLOWERS

Faeries have strong associations with flowers. The flower Faery folk have captured the imagination of many an artist – for instance the illustrations of Cicely Mary Barker's 'Flower Fairies' are enormously popular both with adults and children. Born in 1895 in Croydon, Surrey, England, Cicely Mary Barker spent hours drawing and painting as a child. Due to suffering from epilepsy, she spent a great deal of time at home engaged in her love of painting. Barker is particularly well-known for her 'Flower Fairy' series of books. Her first 'Flower Fairy' book was published in 1923, when Faeries were a very popular topic. Sir Arthur Conan Doyle's book 'The Coming of the Fairies' had been published the year before and included the photographs of the Cottingley Faeries taken by the two young girls Elsie Wright and Frances Griffiths (see page 16). After the success of Barker's first book she wrote seven more. She continued her painting until her eyesight faded towards the end of her life and died in 1973 at the age of 77. Her books are popular throughout the world.

Pillywiggins, otherwise known as 'spring Faeries', are known worldwide. They are found in wildflower fields particularly if there are large oaks around. Pillywiggins are depicted as tiny, playful Faeries with small wings, whose sole purpose is to look after spring flowers. They love to ride bees from flower to flower although their queen, Ariel, prefers bats. She is a blonde, seductive creature of great beauty, who sleeps in a cowslip bed and communicates by singing.

Pixies are also to be found in wildflower fields and flower gardens. They are also known as Piskies, Pisgies, Pigseys, Grigs, Dusters, Pechs and Pickers. They are small creatures with tiny wings, pointed ears, noses, arched eyebrows and heads that appear to be too large for their bodies. They wear little foxglove caps or sometimes toadstool hats and these friendly Faeries love to play and dance.

There are many stories about 'Pixie Dust' which is a silvery-gold powder left behind by their footprints. It is thought that this idea of 'Pixie Dust' may be related to the word 'Picts'. The Picts were early inhabitants of Scotland who worked with gold, silver and bronze. As they walked, the Picts would leave dust behind collected by the soles of their shoes. Thus, 'Picts Dust' became 'Pixie Dust'. It was thought that the Pixies were the spirits of the Picts. Pixies can be very mischievous, unlike Pillywiggins who do not perform tricks on humans. To be led astray by pixies is described as 'pixie-led'.

Flowers particularly associated with Faeries are bluebells, primroses, cowslips, lilies of the valley and foxgloves. If you blow on a dandelion clock the Faeries will make your wishes come true in return for transporting them on their way.

Faeries of the Flowers

From the peak of the irises and wild roses,
The flower Faeries sit and dream
In the beds of water lilies and sweet smelling posies,
These Faeries are the healing team!
And when the day's work is done
Finished is their Faery fun.
The petals close and off they doze,
Don't be forlorn. For when it is dawn
And they have awakened from their Faery sleep,
Out of the petals they will peep,
Looking out of the windows to the world they have created.

CHLOE WHICHELLO

YELLOW FAERIES OF THE FLOWERS

DESCRIPTION

The yellow Faeries are particularly fond of primroses. These beautiful spring flowers are an entrance to Faeryland. One way of opening the door is to touch a Faery rock with a primrose. Another method is to place five freshly gathered primroses on a standing stone. The Irish believe that if you look over primroses in a certain way, the invisible becomes visible and thus the Faeries can be seen. At springtime you should count the number of primroses you first see and if you count 13 or more you will enjoy good luck all year. Some believe that if you lay a posy of primroses on your doorstep as you sleep the Faeries will enter and bless your home.

Cowslips are also Faery flowers and are sometimes known as 'Faery Cups', since the Faery folk like to nestle inside the flowers. The parasol-like clusters of fragrant yellow flowers provide an excellent shelter from the rain.

In 'A Midsummer Night's Dream', Shakespeare writes:

> In their gold coats spots you see:
> Those be rubies, fairy favours:
> In those freckles live their savours.
> I must go seek some dewdrops here
> And hang a pearl in every cowslip's ear.

('A Midsummer Night's Dream', Act 2, Scene 1)

The freckles refer to the five red spots that can be found, one on each petal. It was believed that the 'freckles' in the flower had the ability to remove freckles and other imperfections such as wrinkles and spots from the skin.

Yet another name for the cowslip is 'Key Flower' or 'Key of Heaven'. The pendant flowers suggest a bunch of keys and it was thought that the cowslip could help to find treasure. The cowslip Faeries protect them from being picked as they do not want their Faery gold to be detected. It is unlucky to pick them.

The sunflower is a Faery's favourite 'sun-bed'! Indeed this flower even resembles the radiant golden beams of the sun. The Faeries of the sunflowers love to make you laugh. Faeries also love to dwell in buttercups – if a buttercup makes a yellow glow on your chin then apparently you like butter!

PROPERTIES

The yellow Faeries of the flowers are the Faeries of absolute joy.

Many yellow Faeries are found amongst the first spring flowers and this is their purpose – to put a spring in our step! It is often in springtime that we decide to make changes. We spring clean the house and may even put our house on the market, plan our next exciting holiday or consider buying a new car. The yellow Faeries teach us to hold on to our positivity and dreams and know that our dreams can come true.

The yellow Faeries love to play and are full of fun and laughter. When they are around you, these frolicking floral sprites make you feel like giggling. They are spontaneous and they help you feel young, energetic and invigorated. Don't be so serious about life – try to see the humorous side. If you laugh then your troubles will melt away.

In the springtime try to walk amongst the primroses or simply buy a bowl of daffodils and breathe in the yellow colour of joy.

BLUE FAERIES
OF THE FLOWERS

DESCRIPTION

In flower from early April until the end of May, bluebells form a mass of rich blue colour. Bluebells are another favourite Faery haunt. When the pendulous bell-shaped blossoms ring, they summon the Faeries to their midnight revels and dances. It is considered to be unlucky to pick them.

Children should take particular care when venturing into bluebell glades that are interwoven with Faery enchantments, since they may be held captive. Adults, on the other hand, will be pixie-led and will only find a way out if guided by another mortal.

The Scottish refer to the bluebell as 'Deadmen's Bells' and legend has it that one who hears the ring of a bluebell will soon be dead.

Another blue Faery flower is the delicate forget-me-not. This has the power to unlock Faery treasure and is a symbol of remembrance and true love.

PROPERTIES

The blue Faeries of the flowers exude blue healing energy. Losing yourself in a bluebell wood or in a sea of forget-me-nots will calm and cool your nerves, dispelling any anger and frustration. They are the Faeries of serenity, peace and tranquillity. If you suffer from insomnia, visualise yourself surrounded by their blue healing rays.

The blue Faeries are excellent for anyone who suffers from skin conditions. They help to soothe and cool problems such as eczema, skin redness and irritation.

They are also the Faeries of truth. Venture out into nature and commune with the blue Faeries and they will reveal to you your true nature. They bring clarity and will help you to see a situation clearly. The blue Faeries help ease all disease, whether of mind, body or spirit. Listen carefully for them, for you may hear the tinkling of bells when they're around.

WHITE FAERIES OF THE FLOWERS

DESCRIPTION

The white Faeries of the flowers are particularly fond of the lily of the valley. According to Irish tradition, it forms ladders that Faeries climb when collecting reeds. Indeed one of its synonyms is 'ladder-to-heaven'. The Faeries plait these reeds to make cradles. Widely distributed all over Europe, North America and Northern Asia, the lily of the valley, with its broad leaves and fragrant little, nodding, white, bell-shaped flowers is familiar to everyone. As the buds of purest white open and turn downwards the flowers hang like a pearl of Faery bells.

There are many legends surrounding the lily of the valley. The fragrance is said to draw the nightingale from hedge and bush and lead him to choose his mate. An old Sussex legend tells of the fierce battle fought by St. Leonard, in the woods near Horsham, against a dragon. During this lengthy combat St. Leonard received grievous wounds. Wherever his blood fell, the lily of the valley sprang up. These woods, known as St. Leonard's forest, are still full of a carpet of lilies of the valley.

Water distilled from the flowers was known as 'Aqua-aurea' (Golden Water) and was deemed so precious it was kept in vessels of gold and silver. In an old herbal book called 'Adam in Eden', by William Coles (published in London in 1657), Coles gives details for its preparation and he says of Aqua aurea, 'The wine is more precious than gold, for if any one that is troubled with apoplexy drink thereof with six grains of Pepper and a little Lavender water they shall not need to fear it that moneth.'

Daises are another favourite Faery flower. They are known as a symbol of childhood innocence and are said to originate from a Dryad who presided over forests, meadows and pastures. Roman mythological legend tells us that the nymph Belides, dancing on the turf at the edge of the forest with the other nymphs, caught the eye of Vertumnus, the god of the orchards. To escape his unwanted attention, she transformed herself into the flower bellis, the daisy's botanical name. According to some writers, 'bellis' is derived from the Latin 'bellus', meaning pretty or charming.

In Scotland, the daisy is known as the 'Bairn-wort' meaning child-flower, since children love to collect it to make daisy chains. An old proverb states 'When you can put your foot on seven daisies summer is come'. Daises are also excellent protection against bad Faeries.

Daisy-roots, like dwarf-elder berries, are said to stunt the growth, hence, in English folklore, the Faery Milkah fed Albion, her royal foster-child, on this food to keep him Faery-size!

The delicate flowers of the white jasmine provide the most exquisite Faery perfume. Highly prized by the perfumery trade, the true aroma of jasmine is not exactly reproducible by any artificial means. The intense fragrance of jasmine is intoxicating – many a passer-by cannot resist venturing into the heady realm of the jasmine Faeries. According to folklore, if you dream of jasmine a romance is blossoming.

PROPERTIES

The white Faeries of the flowers symbolise purity, love, innocence and hope. Children have always loved to collect and make necklaces and bracelets from daisies. The daisy is a symbol of their purity and innocence. If you wish to connect with the innocence, go out into a field of daisies and open up your heart to their joy.

The Faeries of the white flowers fill us with hope and positivity. If someone is in despair, perhaps whilst experiencing a serious illness or after bereavement, these Faeries can uplift body, mind and spirit. A small bunch of white flowers often signals the arrival of good news or a change for the better. Always call upon the white Faeries for help if you or someone else feels hopeless or desperate. White flowers are an excellent aid to meditation and may be placed in your special Faery space to draw the Faeries close to you. White jasmine, that is associated with the purity of the Virgin Mary and is known as the 'Star of Divine Hope', is ideal. If you are looking for romance, the jasmine Faeries will attract to you deep affection and loyal love. Essential oil of jasmine is an extremely powerful love potion.

MAUVE AND PURPLE FAERIES OF THE FLOWERS

DESCRIPTION

Foxgloves have a very long association with Faeries. Synonyms include 'Faery's Glove', 'Faery Caps' and 'Faery Thimbles'. The shape of the flowers resembles the fingers of a glove. Foxgloves love to grow wild in deep hollows and woody dells that are, of course, favourite Faery haunts. Not only do Faeries wear foxgloves as gloves, but also as hats. They also use them as thimbles whilst sewing their beautiful outfits. The small flecks on the flowers are the fingerprints of the Faeries. Faeries can also take refuge from the cold and the wet in the foxglove. If a foxglove bows its head it is a sure sign that Faeries are about. An Irish belief is that the juice of ten foxglove leaves will cure a Faery-struck child.

The foxglove, however, is a plant to treat with great caution, not only because of its poisonous nature, but also as it is sometimes associated with bad Faeries! One legend states that Faeries used to give blossoms to the fox to put on his toes so that he would not be heard as he raided the chicken coop. Witches use foxglove juice in potions to help them to fly. It is considered to be unlucky to pick foxgloves from their natural environment for they are Faery dwellings. However, they are lucky if you grow them in your garden from seed.

The sweet-scented violet emerges at the end of February and blooms until the end of April. Violets, like primroses, herald the coming of spring. They are usually deep purple, but lilac or white violets are also found. Legend says that this flower was created by Jupiter as food for his beloved Io after he had changed her into a heifer in a fit of jealousy!

PROPERTIES

The purple and mauve Faeries are beings of great beauty. They are associated with love and the healing of the heart and help to open up this centre, cleanse away any negativity and fill it with optimism.

These Faeries touch the spiritual side of our nature. They awaken and develop out natural intuitive instincts. A posy of violets or flowers of any shade of purple is a wonderful aid for meditation. Deep relaxation is encouraged and intuition is enhanced.

Foxglove

The foxglove bells, with lolling tongue,
Will not reveal what peals were rung
In Faery, in Faery,
A thousand ages gone.
All the golden clappers hang
As if but now the changes rang;
Only from the mottled throat
Never any echoes float.
Quite forgotten, in the wood,
Pale, crowded steeples rise

MARY WEBB

RED FAERIES
OF THE FLOWERS

DESCRIPTION

The rich scarlet petals of the poppy are a Faery-magnet. They love to jump and dance from flower to flower in amongst a field of poppies. These Faeries are full of vitality and joy. They are the wild, mischievous and playful members of the Faery flower kingdom – the life and soul of the party!

Highly adventurous some of the more serene Faery folk despair of them!

PROPERTIES

If you feel tired and jaded then imagine yourself frolicking with the Faeries in a field of poppies. They will fill you with their energy and vitality.

The poppy Faeries are very helpful for those who feel cold, whether on a physical or an emotional level. A tonic for the circulation and extremely restorative, they can bring the sparkle back into your life and warm your heart. Anyone of a nervous disposition should connect with the Faeries of the red flowers. They instil strength and courage and give us the fearlessness to face any challenge, no matter how great!

OTHER FAERIES SIGHTED AMONGST FLOWERS

Faeries are to be found amongst every single flower. Look amongst the pink roses and carnations to discover the Faeries of unconditional love. They can help in all aspects of love and fertility and are very protective towards children and pregnant woman. Go out amongst the orange marigolds and notice how your spirits lift. Amongst the blades of grass the shy Faeries can disappear in a blink of an eye. Look carefully for a four-leaf clover to bring Faery luck into your life and enable you see Faeries! According to legend a milkmaid picked a four-leaf clover together with the grass that she used to soften the weight of the pail on her head. To her astonishment when she looked at her cow, dozens of Faeries were milking it! In Christian folklore, a four-leafed clover is a symbol of the cross and will ward off evil.

CONNECTING WITH THE FAERIES OF THE FLOWERS

I find that the Faeries can pop up in different circumstances. Here are a few ways you might like to try to discover them:

⭐ Go for a walk in a beautiful woodland or garden, walk quietly, listening to the sounds of the elements. Take your time to notice the flowers and plants — make sure you are really relaxed, and rest against a tree or sit in the sun. If a Faery appears then they probably want to work with you. Some places are far more magical than others (especially ancient sites and organic gardens) and once you tune in, lots of Faeries may appear.

⭐ Set up a Faery altar with pictures, candles, flowers and beautiful objects such as crystals. You may wish to write a problem or concern on a piece of paper and put it on the altar. Light a candle and meditate, asking if there is a good Faery that can help with the issue. During the meditation you may get a colour, a plant or flower, name or even 'see' the Faery. Use this information as a basis to dress your Faery.

⭐ Go to a garden centre or florist where they have real and silk flowers. Often a Faery will appear by a flower or flowers that it wants to wear. You may find you are really drawn to certain flowers or colours and these will be the ones your Faery wishes to wear.

⭐ Children are often much more connected to the Faery realms and find it easy to access. Try talking to your children, or those of friends, they can often tell you about the Faeries in your garden or around you.

CREATING YOUR OWN FLOWER FAERY

Whilst writing this book, a Faery friend of mine, Jo Harrington, appeared with the most beautiful Faery flower folk I have ever seen! A small selection of these Faeries is contained within this chapter of the book. I couldn't believe how easy it was to dress my own Faery and was amazed at how connected I felt to the Faery flower kingdom. These are her instructions:

When you dress a Faery of the flowers you are actively bringing their energy into your life. But it is important to connect with their individuality – the last thing you want to do is offend them!

DRESSING A FAERY

Once you have connected with a Faery you need to gather the items for dressing it. The following is just a suggestion to get you started, be as creative as you can.

YOU WILL NEED:

A $\frac{1}{12}$th scale Faery doll or similar doll about 3–5 inches (7–12 cm) in height

Silk flowers

Cotton thread of the same colour

Silk ribbon to match the flowers, in various different widths

Decorative items such as small beads, butterflies, tiny pieces of crystal,

little roses, feathers, stars and sequins

Viscose doll's hair

A 'tacky' glue – there are various water-based glues available from craft and model shops

Fine sewing needles and a selection of knitting needles

Sharp scissors

Begin by taking the flowers apart, removing the plastic stems and centres but leaving the

petals intact. Sometimes the petals are stuck together but they can be carefully prised apart.

Keep the leaves, as they often look lovely as shoes or decoration.

Take a petal, or petals, to form the skirt and

enlarge the centre by making small cuts until you

can pull it onto the doll's waist. If this isn't

possible you may have to cut the petals and sew

a skirt around the doll, using them individually.

Next, make a simple halter top with a piece of silk ribbon tying it at the back.

 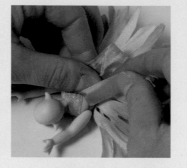 

Decorate the dress with roses and ribbons etc.

Sticking petals, leaves or ribbons around the

feet can make simple shoes. Remember though,

Faeries often have bare feet.

Faery wings can be made from flower petals,

feathers, leaves or fabrics. Cut wing shapes

out of your chosen material and attach to the

back of the halter top.

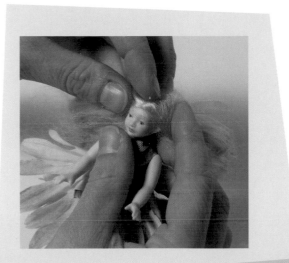

Once dressed, decide on the hairstyle your Faery likes, i.e. wavy, curly, flowing, etc. It is advisable to curl the hair, or even if you require straight hair, to wave it. This makes it more manageable as the hair fibres hold together. Take a section of hair and secure one end to a knitting needle; fine needles produce tight curls or ringlets and larger needles waves. Damp lightly and wind around the needle securing at the other end. Place in a dish. Pour on boiling water and allow to cool. Remove from the dish, leave on the needle and pat off surplus water with a towel. Lay in a warm place until completely dry. Use a tacky glue to attach the hair to the doll. A good tip is to cover the dressed doll loosely in cling film as this protects the clothes whilst wigging your doll.

Once the hair is dry your Faery may like a petal hat or ribbons in its hair. You may also wish to decorate the ears, fingers and toes with little beads.

WATER FAERIES

Water Faeries are abundant in streams, brooks, rivers, springs, wells, ponds, lakes, seas, oceans, fountains, waterfalls and even in raindrops.

Water is associated with healing and also with the release of emotions such as sadness and the transformation that takes place by moving through painful emotions. Deep emotional pain can block the energy of the body and cause many illnesses. Water is a profound healer.

Legends of water spirits are found in many parts in the world:

From Scotland come stories of the Ashrays. These water spirits may be male or female and, despite being ancient, they appear to be only about twenty years old. People mistake them for ghosts, on account of their wisplike translucent bodies. They cannot live on land and they are completely nocturnal, for it is said that they will melt into a pool of water if they are touched by sunlight. The Boobrie is a water bird found in the waters around Scotland and is about a foot high (30 cm) and capable of swimming or flying. It has black feathers, an enormous bill and sharp claws. The Boobrie preys on ships, which are transporting sheep and cattle for meat, its preferred food (it eats fish when none is available). Selkies are found in the ocean and lochs of northern and western Scotland and around the Hebrides. They usually appear as seals but they are able to shed their sealskins and can appear as beautiful young men and women. Some Selkies try to lure humans into the sea. Others come to shore to live as mortals but they soon become bored with their human mates and leave them to pine and die of broken hearts.

In the Black Mountains of Wales, the Gwragedd Annwn can be found near lakes. They are incredibly beautiful, blonde female water Faeries who love children. They like to help women, children and the poor. Gwragedd Annwns love to dance under the full moon. Occasionally they will take humans as husbands and some local families in Wales still claim to be descended from them. If they do marry they make excellent mothers yet distant wives.

The Formorians are said to dwell along the seashores in Ireland. They are sea monsters with grotesque distorted bodies made out of animal parts. They were an early Faery race that conquered Ireland but were banished into the sea by the Tuatha dé Danann (the people of the Goddess Danu). The monstrous Formorians can only leave the sea at night. In the Irish Sea off the coast of the Isle of Man, the Irish Sea Water Guardians can be found. Just a few inches high – both male and female – these small Faeries are a delight to behold as greeny-blue light dances around them. They love to sail on broken eggshells, to surf seashells during stormy weather and play with the dolphins. Irish Sea Water Faeries will help fish and humans, but only if asked. The Bean-Fionn, meaning 'White Woman' is a female Faery living beneath lakes and rivers in Ireland. She reaches out and drowns children who are near or in the water.

The Lorelei inhabits the River Rhine in Germany. She is a beautiful young female Faery who sits on the cliffs and lures sailors to their deaths on the rocks below with her haunting songs. Also found in the River Rhine are the Nixen otherwise known as Nixies who also inhabit other rivers in Germany as well as Switzerland. The female water sprites are very beautiful but the males have green teeth. They invoke storms and lure swimmers and sailors to their deaths on rocks. Nixen are the subject of many German folk songs. Metal can be used against them as a weapon and may even kill them.

In the waters of France we find the Dracs. They naturally look like large purple blobs floating on top of the water but they assume human female form or appear as a golden chalice. By taking on the appearance of a beautiful woman or a golden chalice they attract humans towards them and then grab them, dragging them down under the water to Drac Kingdom. Dracs can also be found in the English Channel. The Corrigans or Korrigans are prevalent in France in the region of Brittany as well as in Cornwall, England. They are found near running water. At night they look like beautiful blonde women but in the day are repulsive old hags. Legends tell of men who marry a Corrigan and are then shocked to discover a hag beside them in the morning! It is said that if a man continues to love a Corrigan during the day then she can become human and be beautiful both night and day.

The waterfalls and fjords of Norway are guarded by the Fossegrim. Smaller than humans these attractive, playful water spirits love to sing and play the harp. The Neck, Neckan or Necker who is also an expert harpist and singer lives in the lakes and streams of Scandinavia. A Neck can shapeshift and make herself very appealing to males to lure them into the water and drown them.

In the waters of Greece particularly, but also near Sweden, can be found the beautiful female water Faeries known as Nereides. They hate children and so they steal them. If milk and honey are left out for them, however, they can be distracted. Nereides are said to have mated with humans on many of the Greek islands. The Undines, otherwise known as Sea Spritos, particularly love to play in the Agean Sea of Greece. Undines look like small seahorses with human faces.

Finally the Merpeople also known as Merman or Mermaids can be found worldwide in the sea, living in sunken wrecks. Their upper bodies are humans and their lower bodies are fish. The Merpeople, both male and female, are beautiful creatures that are usually friendly. Drowning people and sailors can ask for their help.

FAERIES OF WELLS AND SACRED SPRINGS

Faeries who are found around wells and sacred springs are associated with healing properties.
Ancient people have journeyed to these places of pilgrimage in search of cures and blessings for
their ailments. One of the most famous wells I have visited is the Chalice Well at Glastonbury,
England. This is a wonderful place to sit and meditate — it really is a Faery place.

Wells and springs that are found close to sacred hills (Chalice Well is located in a valley between Chalice Hill and the Tor), were associated throughout pre-Christian times with magical properties. Ancient holy wells were cared for by an old wise woman who lived at the well and acted as a healer and counsellor. She would certainly have conversed with the nature spirits.

The source of the water of Chalice Well is unknown and its supply has never run dry, even in the harshest drought. It eventually reaches the Pilgrim's Bath where many acts of healing have been performed. The reddish colour of the water is an interesting feature and is thought to suggest the blood of childbirth or menstruation. It has even been called the Blood Spring because of its colour.

According to one legend Joseph of Arimathea in the 1st century (37 AD or 63 AD, depending on the source) brought the chalice that Jesus drank from at the Last Supper and in which drops of his blood were caught during the Crucifixion, and buried it by the well. Therefore, some believe that the water is mixed with the blood of Christ and that this accounts for its healing properties.

Whatever the truth, many believe in the magical powers of the Chalice Well and even today still visit and drink the water that tastes of iron. Some claim to have been cured of various ailments.

Occasionally when photographs are taken, inexplicable shafts of light can be seen. I find it a wonderful place to sit and ponder — it truly is a Faery haunt.

The chalice well at Glastonbury

DESCRIPTION

The Chalice Well is a place of great tranquillity, peace and harmony. The Faeries inhabiting the well are mostly red and blue in colour. Red Faeries look like feathery red flames as they dart and dash around the stones surrounding the sacred well. They emit warmth and a rush of hot air may be felt if they approach you. You may see them as sparkly red dots or flickering rays of red light.

The blue Faeries are somewhat slower in their movements and resemble flames of ice. A shimmering arc of mist can be felt as they slowly caress you. Take care to always drop in a coin to show respect for the well spirits. Never tease and taunt them. In Irish mythology there is a story of a young woman who aggravated a spirit of a sacred well and she was pulled in!

PROPERTIES

The red Faeries bring energy and rejuvenation – they are particularly beneficial to those suffering with blood disorders such as anaemia. The blue Faeries are endowed with soothing and cooling properties and aid in the healing of inflammatory disorders such as rheumatoid arthritis. They also help to relieve skin conditions where there is itching, irritation or burning. These Faeries also calm the nerves relieving stress and agitation.

The Faery Well

In a garden laden with flowers and a heavenly smell,
The Faeries heal and cure
And in the middle lies a well,
In which water of light stands so still and pure.
This water of love has a gift,
A gift so wonderful it could never be bought
And from it the magical properties
Light into your hands wherever it is caught.
In the whole of your body where you are overcome by the divine power of the Faeries,
And suddenly everything around you, becomes yours.

CHLÓE WHICHELLO

FAERIES OF LAKES AND PONDS

There are many famous legends connecting Faeries with lakes and pools. In Arthurian legend the Lady of the Lake, Vivien, is a Faery. Merlin created a crystal palace for her and masked its appearance in the semblance of a lake so that others would not trouble her. It is said that Vivien will, on rare occasions, allow some individuals to glimpse a reflection of her domain.

DESCRIPTION

The Faeries found in and around lakes and pools are predominately a silvery-blue colour. They have long, slender bodies and glide gracefully through the water, creating hardly a ripple. Creatures of great beauty, they are often to be seen enjoying their exquisite reflections in the clear water.

PROPERTIES

The properties of these Faeries reflect the stillness found in lakes and ponds. Lake and pool Faeries are like a mirror of the soul. They create peace and harmony enabling restless and tormented souls to deal with inner conflicts.

The most beautiful pool that I have ever seen is in the 'Faeries' Mirror' pond, which is found at the 'Valley of No Return' in Brocéliande, Brittany, France. As one gazes into 'Le Miroir aux Fées' (Faeries' Mirror) it becomes hard to distinguish between what is real and what is being reflected. It is a very enchanted place and it is easy to imagine the Faeries staring curiously at their reflections in the clear water.

FAERIES OF THE SEA

In salt water one finds the merfaeries. One must be cautious of these Faeries, since they are unpredictable. There are stories of Faeries who have dragged sailors into the murky depths of the sea and onto the rocks, and others of sea Faeries who have guarded ships safely to shore. There are bad merfaeries as well as good merfaeries.

DESCRIPTION

Merfaeries are various shades of shimmering blue and blue-green. Turquoise is a particularly common colour. They possess tiny, feathery wings and long tails. Some sea Faeries such as Undines, which are Ancient Greek water spirits from the Aegean Sea and resemble sea horses, are small. 'Bad' sea Faeries who create havoc on the sea tend to be larger.

PROPERTIES

The 'good' sea Faeries encourage peace, stillness, contentment and calm. As you stare at the sea they dispel anxiety and tension and they induce an almost trance-like state.

Merfaeries

The day is over yet merfaeries wait,
Watching the ships go by from the rocks
Swimming and diving, although it is late,
Dipping and flashing their sun-kissed locks.

They glide to the bottom of the ocean deep
Where multicoloured fish stare at them blinking,
So human-like yet they have no feet,
But beautiful tails to stop them from sinking.

The merfolk the rulers of oceanous lands,
One with the whales, dolphins and coral
And in the evening they sit on the sands,
Thinking of no particular moral.

CHLÓE WHICHELLO

FAERIES OF BROOKS AND STREAMS

The Faeries who inhabit brooks and streams are young and youthful spirits who radiate joy. They delight in the sound of running water.

DESCRIPTION

They are yellowy-green and blue-green in colour. They move and adapt to the speed of the river. These Faeries are lively and mischievous and if you listen carefully you may even hear them in their joyful antics as they frolic and dance on the banks.

PROPERTIES

They are the bringers of joy of the Faery Kingdom. It is their sense of humour and mischief that makes brooks and streams so attractive to children. They urge us to play like children and fill us with laughter.

Faeries at the Brook
Biding their time by the babbling brook
Sitting, swimming, pondering all night and day
And if you care to steal a look,
Next year, next week, tomorrow today,
You will see them laughing and playing along,
Chanting their secret Faery song.

CHLÓE WHICHELLO

CONNECTING WITH THE WATER FAERIES

★ Go out into nature and find a place with water where you feel safe and you will not be disturbed. Suitable places include a stream, river, brook, well, pond, lake, waterfall, fountain, sea or ocean. If you wish, take a couple of candles with you.

★ Sit or lie comfortably with your back straight and close your eyes.

★ If possible place your hands or feet, or even both, into the water to establish a strong connection with it.

★ Take a few deep breaths — breathe in deeply and release the breath slowly exhaling all your tension.

★ When you feel totally relaxed, ripple the surface of the water several times. Tell the water Faeries either silently or aloud that you wish to communicate with them. As you sense their presence acknowledge them gracefully.

★ As the water gently caresses your body allow the Faeries to take away all of the emotional burdens that you may be carrying. Feel the healing waters removing all the blockages and, if necessary, let the tears flow.

★ Allow the Faeries to send you into a blissfully relaxed state. Thank the water Faeries for sharing their healing energies.

★ When you feel ready to return become aware of your breath once more and open your eyes. You will feel calm and peaceful and so much lighter and clearer than before.

TREE FAERIES

The Tree Faeries

The aspens seem to summon you,
Whispers fill the air,
Springing up from a large yew,
Faeries flutter in the air,
Rowans offer safe protection,
Hazels guide you up the paths,
Willows fill you with affection,
Bringing joy and Faery laughs.
Suddenly, all is hush;
Beautiful birches stand alert and strong,
And everything transforms, radiant and lush
With elegance she glides from the trees,
The forest is listening the birds and bees,
With shimmering light she surrounds us all,
Who thought that such power could come from the small?
The spirit of the birch. The Lady of the Faery Forest.

CHLÓE WHICHELLO

Trees emanate a great power. As we walk through a wood we can feel their strength. Trees fill us with wonder and are a source of inspiration. They give us comfort, peace and a great sense of oneness with nature.

If you take the time to sit beneath a tree you will often receive a message as the tree spirits give you their wise counsel. Indeed, many saints have received their enlightenment whilst meditating under a tree – trees are mediators between heaven and earth and between God and man.

Tree Faeries are a worldwide phenomenon. They have been revered as divine sources of wisdom and even worshipped as deities. The Ancient people believed that trees were sacred and were inhabited by tree spirits. The English poet, novelist and classical scholar Robert Graves in his book 'The White Goddess' (1947), tells of ceremonies for felling trees, warning the tree spirits and asking them for forgiveness. In ancient times, sacred groves, comprised of a group of trees chosen for their particular qualities, were used as places of worship, for meetings, ceremonies and for passing laws and judgments. Many villages even had their own sacred trees that were actually brought into the village. Nowadays, old villages often have a special tree. Ancient people believed that a person's knowledge could be passed on at death and consequently individuals were buried under sacred trees. It was thought that the tree spirits would be able to hold the knowledge and that consequently it would be accessible to the tribe. The long-living yew tree is traditionally planted in graveyards, possibly due to this belief. Some yews are thought to be over 4,000 years old. Important historical meetings have taken place beneath sacred trees, since it was believed that the tree spirit could record the information impartially.

The Celts in ancient Britain are renowned for their veneration of trees. The female Druidic order took its name from the Dryads, otherwise known as Tree Spirits, Tree Ladies, Druidesses or Hamadryads. Celtic Dryads live in all of the 13 Celtic sacred trees many of which will be discussed in this chapter. The Dryads are said to have taught the Druids many secrets, including divination and astral travel. They emerge at night, flitting from tree to tree and singing the most beautiful music. Dryads are referred to as female.

Dryads are also described in Greek mythology – the most famous Greek Dryad was Daphne, who was changed into a laurel tree by Apollo. The Greeks also described male tree spirits known as Drus, as well as Hamadryads, which were tree-bound Faeries who spent their whole lives in one tree.

The Hamadryadniks, who originated in Yugoslavia, are tree spirits disguised as living foliage. They do not like humans, regarding them as destroyers of the forest. They come out in the day, unlike most tree spirits, and at nighttime they must stay in their trees, for if they touch the earth at night they will vanish forever.

The Lesidhe of Ireland also appear as living foliage and strongly disapprove of humans who destroy the environment. Most active at night, they love to confuse travellers with human sounds to lead them in the wrong direction deep into the woods.

The Ghillie Dhu (meaning 'dark shoe') are Scottish tree spirits who are also disguised as foliage. They inhabit birch trees mostly and guard them very protectively. Since they dislike humans, one should take care in Scottish forests that one is not grabbed by the long, green arms of a Ghillie Dhu.

The Scandinavian Hyldermoder is the guardian tree spirit of the sacred elder trees. She is traditionally dressed in a flowing green gown and is like an elderly, protective mother. She is kind to humans unless they try to interfere with the elder tree. Hans Christian Andersen wrote a Faery story called 'The Little Elder-Tree Mother'.

Irish Elves, otherwise known as 'The Little People', are known all over Europe. These Faeries are dwarf-like in appearance and wear green or blue clothes and red caps. They live amongst the tangled roots of sacred trees and are thought to care for wild animals, particularly if the animal is sick.

The children's writer Beatrix Potter mentioned the mischievous Faery Oakmen from Germany and Scandinavia who are male dwarf Faeries with enormous heads and are said to guard sacred oak groves. They are particularly prevalent in the Black Forest of Germany and are not fond of humans.

According to Western European pagan lore, from Yule to Midsummer the Oak King reigns wearing his crown of oak leaves and acorns and carrying a staff of oak wood. At Midsummer, the Holly King takes over as ruler. Interestingly, the robin is the symbol of the Oak King and the wren is the Holly King. The English nursery rhyme, 'Jenny Wren and Robin Redbreast' is evidence of the belief in the Oak King and the Holly King.

The Oak King

The ruler of the forest,
Crown of oak,
Staff of oak,
The robin — the oak king.

Strong as wood,
Hard as oak,
A heart of gold.

Bold,
Protective,
He rules over the forest,
His determination true.

TOM WHICHELLO

MAGICAL TREES

SILVER BIRCH

Description

The most common tree in Scotland and the second-most common tree in English woodland the birch tree is the first tree to colonise new ground. It is often referred to as the 'Lady of the Woods' due to its beautiful slender white trunk and branches. The silver birch is a hardy tree, yet pliable. The sparse foliage allows the light to filter through. It sheds its bark occasionally – in fact, in the past the bark was used for writing on. It is associated with a new start and therefore was traditionally used for babies' cradles. The birch has a reputation for cleansing and driving away evil. These wispy, charismatic Faeries who dwell in birch trees are incredibly beautiful beings with long, slender bodies and arms. These fast-moving Faeries leave a trail of silvery light behind as they dance through the leaves, exhibiting great agility. They are the ladies of the woods – magnificent beings of great purity and elegance.

Properties

The silver birch Faery is energising, revitalising and nourishing. She encourages you to make a fresh start and to take advantage of any opportunities that come your way. She will help you to rid yourself of any unhelpful aspects of your life that may be hindering your progress. Just as the birch sheds her bark, so you too can shed your old patterns.

ROWAN

DESCRIPTION

The rowan tree, also known as mountain ash, grows at a higher altitude than any other broad-leaved tree in the most inaccessible areas and grows best in north and western Scotland where it is known as the 'Lady of the Mountains' (it was named the 'Whispering Tree' because the ancients thought the tree held secrets). Its wood is yellow-grey and the berries of the rowan tree are a flaming orange-red. The rowan tree was considered to be highly effective against evil enchantments.

The rowan berry has a tiny five-pointed star known as a pentagram opposite its stalk and is an ancient magical symbol of protection. A rowan twig was tied to a cow's tail to prevent the Faeries from stealing milk; cradles were carved out of rowan to protect babies from being stolen; crosses made of rowan were tied on barns, with red twine, on May morning to ward off bad Faeries; 'bewitched' horses were tamed by using a whip made of rowan; rowan was hung in cattle sheds to protect the animals from harm; in Wales, rowan was planted in graveyards to ensure peaceful rest for the dead.

The rowan is connected with the Celtic goddess Brigid who lights the fire of inspiration, divination and healing. According to legend, Brigid was born with a flame coming out of the top of her head connecting her with the universe. The new (Christian) and the old (pagan) Brigid were merged into St. Brigid in 450 AD. St. Brigid, daughter of a Druid, was a healer and goldsmith. In Kildare, Ireland, her sacred fire can be found, which is guarded by nineteen priestesses/nuns. On the twentieth of each month it is said she appears and tends it herself.

The rowan tree Faery is bursting with energy and her red flames of fire can be seen as red rays of light darting through the rowan tree. Her eyes are like the brightest rubies that fill you with energy, motivation and inspiration. As she surrounds you with a circle of fire, to protect you from negative forces, and lights a fire on the top of your head, you feel warmth and a tingling. You feel energised, protected and inspired.

PROPERTIES

The rowan Faery will protect you against harmful influences so that you can ward off any negativity, or emotional or psychic attack. Try to spend time with the rowan trees. Place a piece of rowan in your pocket or in a small pouch to carry around with you, or put a spray on your bedside table or hang it over your door if you feel vulnerable.

The rowan Faery can also enhance your intuition and increase your psychic powers. You may receive visions of events to come. Trust your insights and intuition.

Rowan will inspire you with ideas and motivation and light up the pathway before you.

Finally she will increase your vitality and encourage you to hold on to your beliefs and not to give up.

The Rowan Faery

The lady of the mountain
Lies silent and still,
Until springing to life like a fountain,
Her ruby red eyes flashing like jewels in the night,
Banishing the terror and fright
And showering the world with guidance and protection.
Newfound wisdom is yours,
Dreams become clear,
Opened are doors,
The future is here.

CHLÓE WHICHELLO

WILLOW

DESCRIPTION

Dryads dwell in willows in preference to all other trees. Willow trees, are said to move around at night in order to find new locations to lay down their roots.

The willow is sacred to the Moon Goddess and the tree-dwelling spirits are most active at full moon. The willow Faery is a slender, sleek and supple tree-dweller with a moon-shaped face, who has an affinity for movement, whether it be physical or emotional. She is an adaptable being who loves to weave her way through the branches of the willow and moves at night, especially when the moon is full. The willow lady loves us to express our emotions, whether we laugh or cry. When the moon is full she is nurtured by the moon's silver light and she delights in shining her beams of light in the darkness to illuminate the path before us.

PROPERTIES

The willow is a water-seeking tree associated with the female side of our nature. Therefore it encourages us to keep in touch with our emotions and also to release them. The willow energy allows deeply buried emotions to come to the surface and be resolved. Only through the process of moving through our deep emotional pain can we move on and become healed. It has been used as a symbol of grief and the willow Faery shows us the importance of moving through the various stages of sadness and expressing our grief through trees. If a branch of a willow tree becomes disconnected it can easily grow into a new tree. Thus, the willow Faery teaches us that from a loss can come new growth and healing.

Willow bark is an old herbal remedy that reduces fever and relieves rheumatism and arthritis. Interestingly the bark of the willow tree contains salicin, which is converted to salicylic acid in the body and has been used for its pain-relieving qualities since ancient times. Salicylic acid is closely related to the synthetic drug aspirin, which has displaced willow bark from popular use.

The willow also urges us to follow and trust our intuition. It enhances visions and a willow leaf placed under the pillow increases dreams and also enables you to interpret your dreams. In the dream state many emotional tensions are released and thus healing can take place.

Willow twigs are very pliant. This made it a popular material for basket making. Its flexible twigs show us not to resist but to move with the flow of life.

The Willow Faery

The night is dark, the moon is bright
And stars shine like torches in the night;
The willow Faery waves her silvery wand
And her hair cascades down, long tresses so blonde;
Our sorrow, happiness come to the fore,
Our emotionless days bring trouble no more,
We no longer resist, we go with the flow of the wind and water
And run wild, dancing in the moonlit beams,
Which she bestows upon us, gifts from the heavens
And the stars glimmer down, watching her in their millions.

CHLÓE WHICHELLO

OAK

DESCRIPTION

The oak provides the richest habitat of any tree for insects. It is a very slow-growing tree and only produces acorns after forty years. However, it has a lifespan of centuries and there are many ancient and famous oaks. The oak was very sacred to the Druids, who met beneath it. The oak tree is often called the 'King of the Forest'. Even when struck by lightening it still survives. As it lives to a great age it often splits open, creating an ideal spot for communing with the oak men who dwell in these trees.

Oak men are the colour of the trees they inhabit. The eyes of the oak men are deep and brown and are full of strength and wisdom. One can feel the power of these ancient tree spirits from a great distance. They are at least as large as the trees that they inhabit.

PROPERTIES

Oak was used in the construction of boats and ships and for the frames of churches on account of its strength and durability. The mighty oak men fill us with the strength and courage necessary when facing great difficulties. They give us back our will to fight that may have become weakened in stressful times.

If you sit beside an oak tree you can absorb the ancient wisdom of the oak men and find deep peace and solace as they embrace you. They teach us the lesson of patience – what is the point of hurrying and becoming stressed? The oak men also remind us of the importance of remaining earthed and grounded.

The Oak Men
Their creaking branches filled with power,
Their faces a bundle of wrinkles
And still their beauty is as sweet as a flower
Except rough, strong, majestic and all around the forest crinkles
And they watch, so still, their brown eyes ablaze with the colours of the forest,
So knowing and filled with such patience that lasts throughout the passage of time.

CHLÓE WHICHELLO

HOLLY

DESCRIPTION

The evergreen holly tree is very much associated with Christmas celebrations, when it is made into wreaths and used extensively for decorating our houses.

It was considered unlucky to cut down holly trees. They are thought to protect you against thunder, lightening and evil.

Holly-tree spirits are dark emerald green with spiky hands and feet, which protect the trees from harm. Their eyes are red, staring and piercing. Holly-tree dwellers are very masculine and pulsating with potent life energy. Their leaves are a symbol of everlasting life.

PROPERTIES

Holly is a potent energiser that stimulates us into action. It awakens our senses and is excellent for restoring direction to our lives when we have lost our way. Holly counteracts negative thought patterns such as hatred, anger, jealousy and revenge that can be so debilitating. If you are or have been emotionally drained, ask the spirit of the holly tree to cut through the ties that are binding you together. This will enable you to move on and regain your balanced power.

The Holly Faery

Hatred, jealousy, revenge, lightening and evil
Suddenly vanish under the snow,
So pure and white,
Apart from the evergreen holly tree,
A striking green on a blank canvas.
Everlasting life, a symbol of hope through the desolate coldness
And all around, Faery snowflakes flutter through the ice-blue sky,
Spreading misty warmth around the blanket of snow, which is not warm but cold
And many life forms sleep never to be disturbed again
Their spiky hands and feet pad against the snow;
Their red eyes staring through the mist, knowing and watching.

CHLÓE WHICHELLO

IVY

DESCRIPTION

Ivy has a destructive aspect and has the ability over a period of time to smother and kill any tree. It can also bind trees together, thereby restricting and impeding one's passage through the woods. As it spreads from one tree to another it unites them together.

   The ivy Faery is a very determined and powerful tree dweller. Her hair is wild and unkempt as she wanders from one tree to another. She has many arms, which are like long tentacles to enable her to wrap herself around trees. Her hands and feet are suckers that bind and entwine.

PROPERTIES

The realm of the ivy Faery is extensive and she encourages us to explore and roam freely, in order that we may discover our true self. In our wanderings we may discover parts of ourselves that we were not aware of. Explore new territory and try new things, but do not wander round aimlessly.

   The ivy Faery urges us not to cling to old habits, patterns or attitudes that restrict our freedom. Do not attach yourself to one concept but instead embrace all concepts.

The Ivy Faery

She wades through the woods, her hair astrewn
And clings to trees which stand so tall,
Causes plants to meet their doom,
Oh, such a burdrn takes its toll,
Paths are slashed to passers-by.
And with a wink of jade-green eye,
Her tentacles like arms reach out through heather
And bind unsuspecting plants together,
So though she may seem so cruel.
Appearing that way to a fool,
Her aiding ways encourage us not to cling,
But be yourself, frolic, dance and sing,
Discover new territories and paths,
Let your life be filled with faery laughs,
Don't restrict your concepts, embrace new ones, be unpredictable,
Be you!

Chlóe Whichello

ASPEN

DESCRIPTION

The aspen is often called the whispering, or talking, tree. It grows by sending out suckers, which can become new trees. One aspen tree can generate many trees that are all joined together at the roots.

The sylph-like aspen Faery quivers and whispers to you in the wind, gently reminding you to listen to your inner voice. Aspen is a silvery-white Faery of great beauty and purity who has long slender arms that soar up to the heavens. A Faery of great peace and love, she lifts away all our worries and fears.

PROPERTIES

The message of the aspen Faery is to learn to listen to and trust one's own inner voice. We should take notice of any messages and act upon them fearlessly.

She tells us that we have nothing to fear, for wherever we go we are loved and supported. There is no danger. The aspen Faery helps us to release our deepest fears, whatever they may be – fear of death, fear of pain and suffering or fear of being alone. We are all connected to the source of love.

The Aspen's Message

A tickle of comfort touches your ear,
Though it may be the only one you can hear,
A voice of beauty, pure and love,
Soft and delicate, a cashmere glove,
"You have nothing to fear," the voice caresses,
"Listen to your heart and embrace your soul,
Don't hide away from the world as a mole."
Love and support is wherever you go,
Turn your back to evil's crow,
We are all connected to love's source,
Though some are exposed to a wicked force,
Dismissive of love and drenched in sorrow
And a feeling there will be no tomorrow,
But listen to this, every day
Is one that should be cherised in many a way,
Opportunities are great, should not be missed
And with that she departed and kissed
My cheek.

CHLÓE WHICHELLO

YEW

DESCRIPTION

Yew trees grow best on limestone and chalk soils. They grow very slowly and have an extraordinarily long life. Yew trees can be thousands of years old – the age of a yew may be determined from the girth of its trunk that increases by a foot every thirty years. They have survived the climatic changes of our planet, as evidenced by fossils dating back 140 million years.

The yew tree is a common feature of many churchyards and ancient burial places. Celtic elders and leaders were often buried beneath a yew so that their knowledge and wisdom would be passed to the tree and therefore be available to the tribe in the future.

The yew grows in a most unusual way, since its branches grow down into the ground to form new stems, which become the trunks of new trees. When the trunk of the original tree becomes old and decays, a new tree can grow from out of the old tree trunk. Since the new tree is feeding from the same roots, it is the process of rebirth and everlasting life that the yew tree teaches us.

The very attractive, deep golden timber is easy to carve. Its combination of a hard heart and a springy outer wood armed English archers with the famous longbow. Weapons made of yew can be found in museums everywhere. A 90,000-year-old yew spear was discovered in Germany between an elephant's ribs!

The bark, foliage and seeds within the fruit are all poisonous. This is one of the reasons that some refer to the yew as the 'Death Tree'.

The nature spirit of the yew tree is a beautiful deep-golden brown. Although she is very ancient and wise the yew Faery has the appearance of a very young woman, since she is continuously transforming and regenerating. Her heart is full of unconditional love and she wears a cloak of magnificent yew leaves. She moves with dignity like a Queen of the Forest.

PROPERTIES

The yew tree represents the processes of rebirth and transformation. She shows us that death is merely a part of the cycle of life. Out of the old can come the new. The yew Faery teaches us the importance of growth – physical, mental, emotional and spiritual. We must learn to release without resistance – to let go of the old life to move forward into the new. The yew tree has always been regarded as a direct link with our ancestors. It helps us to remember that we can connect with other levels of existence.

The Yew Tree

Underneath the boughs of an old yew tree,
An ancient master sleeps,
His flesh is gone, bones crumbled like chalk,
But wisdom still he keeps;
The yew tree possesses his spirits, his soul,
In its deep, golden timber
And passes down the information
From old to the new,
Whispering secrets in the wind,
The fruit is so tempting
Yet deadly.
If you were to eat it you would have all the information on this earth,
But . . . .you would be dead, silent, like the hushed noiselessness of the yew.

CHLÓE WHICHELLO

HAWTHORN

DESCRIPTION

The hawthorn, whitethorn or May Tree, a beautiful, thorny little tree, which can live to a great age and grows in the wildest of spots, is rich in folklore. This enchanted tree, known as the 'Faery tree', flowers in the month of May. The word May is derived from the Greek Goddess Maia who cast spells with hawthorn. Hawthorn was used for May Day celebrations to decorate maypoles and make garlands as a symbol of renewed life and sexual union. It is said that one should take care not to sit under a hawthorn tree on May Eve otherwise the Faeries will enchant you. According to folklore, the spirit of the hawthorn was capable of being vindictive if it was cut or interfered with in any way. The cattle of a farmer who demolished a hawthorn perished and his children died one by one, while two Irish brothers who felled hawthorns on a burial mound 'lost their luck' – one brother was 'Faery-struck so badly nothing would cure him'.

It was considered unlucky to bring flowering hawthorn inside, as it would bring death to the house. The 13th-century Scottish poet, Thomas the Rhymer, who was believed to have vanished into Faeryland for seven years, warned neighbouring villagers to look after their hawthorn well:

As long as the Thorn Tree stands
Erceldoune shall keep its land

The Eildon Tree, Thomas' favourite, by the waterfall, remained standing until as late as 1814, when it was blown over in a storm, but the spot is marked. The villagers tried to revive it by pouring whisky over its roots, but to no avail. The prophecy proved correct. A chain of financial disasters struck the village and it had to sell off its common land to pay its debts.

The Glastonbury Thorn also referred to as the 'Holy Thorn' is found in England. The legend goes that soon after the death of Christ, Joseph of Arimathea came to Britain to spread the message of Christianity. When he travelled there from the Holy Land with his twelve companions they were all very weary. Joseph thrust his staff made of hawthorn into the ground and it took root, began to grow and blossom. A tree grown from one of the original cuttings can still be seen in the grounds of Glastonbury Abbey today. It flowers twice a year at Christmas as well as in May. A sprig of the blossom is sent to the reigning monarch every year at Christmas. Many consider the Glastonbury Thorn to be a holy tree and claim that it has healing abilities. Solitary hawthorn trees growing on hills or near sacred wells serve as markers to the Faery realm.

The hawthorn Faeries are wild and enchanting. They wear garlands of blossom in their hair and are full of energy. Their long hair swirls wildly around as they dance around with the light of love. You will feel a surge of warmth in your heart or you may feel a Faery touch on your cheek or lips.

And therefore hath the
white thorn many virtues!
For he that bearest
on hym thereof,
non manner of
Tempest may dere him:
be in the hows
that yt is ynne
may none evil ghost entre.

('THE TRAVELS OF SIR JOHN MANDEVILLE', 1350)

PROPERTIES

The message of the hawthorn Faeries is to open up your heart and love. They enable us to let go of fear to make way for the energy of all. There are many kinds of love, for example, brotherly, sisterly, parental and friendly – all love should be unconditional. We should try to open our hearts to the giving and receiving of love.

Hawthorn can also be used on a physical level for heart problems. Hawthorn berries provide one of the best herbal tonics for the heart and circulatory system. They are used in herbalism for palpitations, high blood pressure and angina. Other trees that are particularly magical where Faeries gather include the ash, elder, alder, hazel and broom. Of course nature spirits are found in every tree.

Hawthorn

In the merry month of May,
The Goddess Maia casts her spells.
If a mortal were to stray
Under a hawthorn on May Eve,
They would hear tinkling of Faery bells.
If cut or harmed in any way,
On humans, Faeries take their wrath,
Decrease their numbers the little ones may,
And send them up their heavenly path.

The hawthorn Faeries run wild and free,
They tell you to find the key to your heart;
Messages of affection, they make you see,
From them you'll never bear to part.

CHLÓE WHICHELLO

CONNECTING WITH THE TREE FAERIES

Tree Faeries have very magical and powerful energy fields that can radiate out for large distances. As we approach trees we can receive their balanced flow of healing energy, either consciously or not. Try this exercise to communicate with the Faery tree spirits:

Find a Faery tree — one of the ones mentioned in this chapter is particularly recommended. A bright, moonlit night is favoured by the Faeries.

Approach your chosen tree slowly and quietly with your heart open.

Once you are standing under the tree observe the moonlight as it filters and dances through the trees. Try to become aware of any Faeries moving amongst the branches, twigs, leaves and blossoms.

Move closer and touch the trunk of the tree to feel its energy pulsating through you.

Now sit down with your back against the tree and relax and tune into the tree more deeply. Close your eyes and breathe in the energy and the qualities of the spirit of the tree. Release any negativity into the ground. Stay there for as long as you like.

Stand up and feel as if you have strong roots like the trees. Let the earth force flow through you until you are nourished, strong and calm.

Thank the Faery tree spirits for sharing their energy with you.

Move slowly away from the tree and enjoy the sense of peace and oneness with nature that you have attained.

SACRED-SITE FAERIES

Sacred sites have always been a great source of fascination for me. I have visited many ancient

sites over the years and indeed have revisited some on many occasions. Each time my awareness

increases, aspects previously hidden reveal themselves to me and the magical energies stir my soul.

Growing numbers of individuals are being drawn to sacred ancient sites. I urge you to explore

such sites and I can guarantee that you will sense the mystery and power that surrounds them.

Let me share with you some of my experiences of the magical beings that dwell in these places.

BRITTANY — FRANCE

The ancient stones and stone circles in Brittany are guarded by the Korreds otherwise known as Korrs or Kores. They are described as elven-like creatures that have hairy bodies, spindly arms and legs, cloven feet, cat's claws and dark skin. Their heads are large with red eyes, long, pointed noses and spiky hair. The male creatures carry leather purses containing hair and scissors and their voices are rough and cracked. The females are hardly ever seen.

The Korreds are not only Faery guardians of the dolmens (stone monuments thought to be tombs) and standing stones, Faery lore claims that they actually carried the stones on their backs and erected them. They either live beneath them, in caves, or under sea cliffs.

Korreds love to dance and they leave a circle burnt in the grass. Any man who is pulled into the circle is whirled around until he dies of exhaustion, whereas a woman will give birth to a child that looks like a man she has never slept with!

However, the Korreds can be kind to humans. If you leave a tool such as a scythe or a knife by the stones with a small payment you will find it has been sharpened in the morning.

The Korreds look very fierce, but this is necessary as their task is to protect the stones and frighten away humans who try to desecrate the stones. They despise humans who claim to seek spiritual enlightenment but do so to boost their egos and personal power. They are unusual in that they have no fear of iron whereas most Faeries do.

MENHIR DU CHAMP DOLENT, DOL-DE-BRETAGNE, BRITTANY

Approximately 3 miles (2 km) to the south of Dol is found the imposing granite Menhir du Champ Dolent which is around 30 feet (9.5 m) high. It is therefore one of the largest menhirs (single upright stone) in Brittany. Legend says that it sprang up in the middle of two armies to stop the two leaders, who were brothers, from fighting. The menhir is thought to sink one inch (25 mm) every century and legend states that its disappearance will coincide with the end of the world.

Menhir du Champ Dolent, Brittany

When I visited this megalith in 2001, the energy it emitted was so immense that visitors did not dare to venture near the stone. They gazed upon it at the roadside. It was as if the mighty Korreds had created a protective force field all around the menhir. I approached this magnificent stone with an open heart and asked if I might be allowed to touch it. Breton legends state that the Korreds will help any sincere spiritual seeker who comes to share the power of the stone. I felt the energy change almost as if the Korreds had created a pathway to the menhir for me. I did not feel at all threatened or fearful. I felt moved and privileged to be able to share in the power of this ancient stone. As I made a physical connection with the stone I felt an immense protective energy surge through my entire being. The Korreds at the Menhir of Champ Dolent were truly magnificent beings of great strength and stature who guard the stones from those who would desecrate them.

THE GREAT ALIGNMENTS, CARNAC, BRITTANY

Carnac contains the world's largest collection of megalithic monuments and attracts thousands of visitors every year. The alignments at Carnac stretch over a distance of almost 9 miles (15 km) from Erdeven in the west to La Trinité-sur-Mer in the east. These monuments were built around 4,000 to 3,000 BC. The beautiful group of alignments at Ménec marks the beginning of the Carnac series. The second set, the Kermario Alignment, has ten to twelve lines of 982 menhirs. The third set of alignments is Kerlescan and are comprised of thirteen rows of stones. The Petit Ménec Alignments are often missed by tourists as most stop only at the principle site. Unfortunately, parties of tourists have caused erosion and worked the menhirs loose, therefore they have been mostly fenced off by the French heritage agency. The Petit Ménec stand hidden in woodland and a path winds through a somewhat marshy area. They include over one hundred small stones in eight main rows.

The Ménec Alignments at Carnac, Brittany

On a recent visit to Carnac I was disappointed when I arrived at the Ménec Alignments to see them fenced off. I 'knew' that I was supposed to visit this series that signals the beginning of the great alignments, as well as the Petit Ménec Alignments. I asked the keepers of the Carnac stones, the stone Faeries or Korreds whom I had previously encountered at the Menhir du Champ Dolent, if I may be permitted to enter. I was immediately drawn around to the back of the alignment. My companion was somewhat surprised at the pathway I was taking around the backs of houses and through fields and made remarks such as, "I think I've just seen a sign 'Beware of the dog!'" But I was not deterred, felt no fear and knew instinctively that I was going in the right direction. To my surprise, I found a gate open to the alignments – it was as if the Faery guardians were calling to me. The rows of menhirs welcomed me in and I felt as if they wanted to teach me the lessons of the stones. I placed my back against one of the menhirs and was allowed to draw in the energy. I connected them with all the other ancient sites I have visited and in particular the Great Pyramid of Giza in Egypt. Although I was only in the Ménec Alignment for 20 minutes or so it was as if I had been in their energy for a lifetime. I gracefully gave thanks to the gentle giant, stone-Faery guardians of Ménec.

I then went to visit the often forgotten rows of megaliths – Le Petit Ménec. To reach it one must go into the woods and it can be swampy. However, since the tourists ignore this alignment it is not yet fenced off. It was wonderful to enter such a sacred place and to spend some time with these majestic stones that have been left so undisturbed lurking in the forest. As you enter Le Petit Ménec it is easy to slip into a meditative state and draw in the power and the beauty of this ancient site. The stone-Faery guardians here were some of the gentlest I have ever encountered. There was no need for them to be on the defensive, for humans do not often venture in to disturb them. They had an almost feminine energy that filled you with a warm glow and nurtured your inner being. There were no scary Faeries here!

The Rock of the Faeries, Brittany — a sanctuary of peace and wisdom

THE ROCK OF THE FAERIES, ESSÉ, BRITTANY

Faeries have played a large part in legends of megaliths. La Roche aux Fées is the most celebrated and is one of the most beautiful dolmens in France. A dolmen is a megalithic monument built of stone slabs and is thought by many to be a tomb. The Rock of the Faeries is constructed of slabs of red, Cambrian shale. Naturally, the Faeries are said to have transported the enormous blocks in their aprons and dropped a few on the way!

Interestingly the tree at the entrance to La Roche aux Fées has a very ancient appearance and is fascinating to behold in its own right. This 'Faery tree' provides a perfect Faery dwelling, with its countless nooks and crannies, and is teeming with nature spirits. How ever do they all manage to fit in there? As you enter the dolmen there are two enormous Faery guardians, larger than the slabs of stone, who graciously allow sincere humans to pass. Enter the dolmen with reverence, for this is a spiritual sanctuary. This is a place to sit undisturbed and share the peace and wisdom of these magnificent stones. It has an exceptional aura of sanctity and engenders a sense of calm and repose.

ENGLAND

CORNWALL

Cornwall is an area rich in standing stones. There are nearly ninety in the Land's End peninsula alone. The Faeries that guard the ancient stones of Cornwall are known as 'Pyrenees'. There are many legends surrounding the ancient stones of Cornwall. One legend claims that the stones can rise up, walk, dance and sing! Although no one has actually ever seen a Pyrenee, their energy is particularly evident in the megaliths of Cornwall at nighttime.

One place to find them is the Trethevy Quoit, north of Liskeard. The term 'quoit' is often applied to dolmens in Cornwall. This is one of the most impressive ones in Britain and due to its height of 15 feet (4.5 m) is referred to by locals as the 'Giant's House'. This dolmen has a strange doorway and a mysterious porthole on its capstone. The giant stone Faery that inhabits this house is certainly very protective of his dwelling – make sure you ask his permission to enter!

Pendeen Vau is a 'figou' – a subterranean stone-lined passageway. The function of these underground passageways is unknown but it is likely they were used for ceremonial purposes. There are many legends surrounding the mysterious Pendeen Vau. Some have speculated that there is buried treasure there. At the entrance stands a beautiful female Faery – the White Lady. She dresses in white and at the winter solstice appears at the entrance of the figou with a red rose in her mouth. According to one legend, the White Lady will transform into a horrific entity if she is followed into the figou.

The Cheesewring on the southern edge of Bodmin Moor, is a series of giant flat boulders some of which are over 30 feet (9 m) in circumference. According to Cornish folklore it was Giants who put them there. The Giants thought that the Saints were receiving much more attention than they themselves were, and the annoyed Giants met on Bodmin Moor to decide upon a course of action. St. Tue, a rather diminutive Saint, heard them arguing and challenged their strong leader Uther to a rock-throwing contest! St. Tue promised that if the Giants won the Saints would leave Cornwall forever, but if they lost they would convert to Christianity. Twelve large flat rocks were gathered together in readiness for the competition. Uther, a champion rock-hurler, hurled the first rock a hundred feet (30 m) or so onto the summit of Stowes Hill. St. Tue, with heavenly assistance, threw the second rock onto the first rock. The competition continued until Uther failed with the last rock. St. Tue hurled it, with the help of the angels, onto the top of the stones and it balanced perfectly. The Giants under Uther now abandoned their sinful ways. The Cheesewring is a reminder of the struggle between the Giants and the Saints.

Many legends say that it was the Giants who built the megalithic monuments. Giants are a big feature of children's Faery tales and are usually depicted as unfriendly or evil. Possibly because of their size, Giants have been regarded as unpleasant, but they can be friendly and welcome human interaction. The giant stone Faeries that are the guardians of the Cheesewring are very gentle, likeable characters full of fun and playfulness.

The Mên-an-Tol near the village of Madron, Penzance, on the Land's End peninsula is an extraordinary monument consisting of four stones: one fallen, two uprights, and between these a circular one, 4ft 6in (1.3 m) in diameter, pierced by a hole that occupies about half its size. It is known locally as the Crickstone for it has the power to cure a crick in the

Many legends say giant stone Faeries built megalithic monuments

back. Legend suggests that anyone with a health problem should crawl through the hole in the centre of the stone nine times. For centuries children suffering from rickets were passed naked through the hole three times. The act of emerging from the stone symbolises rebirth from the womb of the Mother Earth. You return healed and the disease is left in the Underworld. The three stones of Mên-an-Tol represent male and female powers. Many marriages took place at these stones – the couple would hold hands through the stone to pledge their everlasting love. The holed stone is also a symbol of fertility and small holed stones were carried as fertility charms as well as for protection and healing. A holed stone may be placed under the pillow for protection against nightmares. According to the ancients, holed stones are a symbol of the female, the Goddess energy, and any holes in the ground such as caves and wells symbolise the womb of the Earth Goddess. The energy at Mên-an-Tol is predominately female – gentle, nurturing and protective.

If you go to Mên-an-Tol or indeed any other holed stone look carefully for stones are a gateway to other worlds. Look closely and you will be able to gaze upon the worlds of Faeries completely protected from harm.

STONEHENGE

Stonehenge is undoubtedly one of the most famous megalithic monuments in the world. It is also a favourite Faery haunt. No one knows exactly how it was built and by whom and so there are many legends attached to Stonehenge. Some say the stones were put in place by Merlin whilst others claim they are giants dancing who were suddenly and without reason turned into stone. I can see why this legend is popular, as the shape of the megaliths rather resembles the shape of giants holding hands. Many are of the opinion that Stonehenge has magical healing properties. Unexplained phenomena occur fairly commonly at Stonehenge – witnesses report seeing strange beams of light and hearing peculiar noises emanating from the stones.

Stonehenge, England

Unfortunately, due to erosion caused by vast numbers of visitors, Stonehenge has been fenced off to the public. I have been lucky enough to visit the stones on several occasions in private parties and therefore have been able to touch and sense the power of the stones. As you walk around the massive stones (some weigh 26 tons/26,417 kg) you are filled with a sense of mystery and are almost stunned into silence. The stone Faeries that guard Stonehenge walk through the sacred archways silently and with reverence. These stone Faeries have the appearance of giant monks. As they walk through the stones they leave their imprints. The Stonehenge guardians are full of wisdom and are ready to impart their secrets to those who will listen quietly and carefully to their whispers.

ROLLRIGHT STONES, OXFORDSHIRE

The Rollright Stones, just north of Chipping Norton, Oxfordshire, are a famous group of prehistoric megalithic monuments. There is a legend that these ancient standing stones were guarded by a witch. A king and his army were marching across the Cotswolds when they encountered this witch. She said to the King:

'Seven long strides thou shalt take!
If Long Compton thou canst see,
King of England thou shalt be!'

On the King's seventh stride the ground rose up before him thus obscuring his view of the village. They were all turned into stone by the witch – the King became the 'King Stone', his men became the 'King's Men Stone Circle' and his five knights became the 'Whispering Knights'.

The witch then transformed herself into an elder tree close to the stones so that she could watch over the countryside and ensure her spell was not broken. On Midsummer Eve, it was customary to go to the King Stone, feast and then cut the elder tree to bring fertility to the land. Unfortunately, the tree has been cut down due to vandalism but there are bushes of elder near the King Stone. Although the legend speaks of a 'witch' she was in fact the 'Hyldermoder'. She is the guardian of the sacred elder trees. She appears as an elderly and protective mother. The Elder Mother is kind towards humans except that permission must be sought before picking her berries.

GLASTONBURY TOR

The magnificent Tor has long been recognised for its sacred power. Some believe that it is possibly the most powerful site in the United Kingdom. This spiritual landmark rises 522 feet (159 m) above the surrounding landscape. Thousands of visitors feel compelled to climb to the top of this holy hill every year. It is a fairly easy climb and from the top you will be astonished at the stunning views. On a misty day one can imagine what it was like when Glastonbury was an island – the Isle of Glass. You can either walk straight up to the top or follow the spiralled Tor labyrinth that winds its way around the hill. Many believe the terraces encircling the Tor are the remains of an ancient three-dimensional labyrinth that was probably used for initiation rituals. Worshippers would have walked along the labyrinth to reach the summit where the Goddess was believed to reside.

The Tor has many names – the Faeries' glass mountain, the magic mountain, spiral castle, Grail castle, an Arthurian hillfort or a magnetic power point.

There are many myths associated with Glastonbury that are still very much alive today. The Tor is traditionally the entrance to the underworld – Annwn. It is also the home of Gwyn ap Nudd who is the King of the Faeries. Annwn is the enchanted underworld to which human souls travel at death. There is no sickness in Annwn and one never grows old there. The fountains run with wine and its inhabitants spend their days feasting and drinking. The underworld is ruled by Gwyn ap Nudd, Welsh Lord of the Dead and King of the Faeries. He is the ruler of the Tylwyth Teg, or Fair Family, small Welsh Faeries with fair hair. They live in clan groups and the eldest male is the primary defender of the clan, like the ancient Celts of Wales. The Teg's children mature at one hundred years old when they leave home to find mates and set up communities of their own. At one time they were accused of stealing children, especially ones with fair hair and skin. They would substitute them for ugly changelings but they no longer do this. They come out at night in search of food and fresh water. Tylwyth Tegs live on Faery islands off the Welsh coast that are connected to the mainland by tunnels. They are harmless until their islands are invaded. Their islands are full of the choicest fruits and beautiful flowers.

Gwyn ap Nudd's underworld can be reached either beneath Glastonbury Tor or through the Welsh lakes. According to legend the Faery King summoned Collen, a Welsh saint of 650 AD, to a meeting at noon at the summit of the Tor and, after many refusals, he finally went to meet the King of the Faeries. Saint Collen had objected to Gwyn ap Nudd being referred to as the King of the Faeries and King of the Underworld. He secretly took a vial of holy water in his robes for protection against the 'devils'. On the hilltop, Collen found the most beautiful castle he had ever seen surrounded by the people of Gwyn's court. A courtier told him that the king was waiting to eat inside the castle and Collen walked in. King Gwyn, seated on a golden throne, in his glittering palace, greeted him and invited him to partake of the banquet but Collen would not eat the Faery food. When the king tried to draw Collen's attention to the beauty of his soldiers and courtiers and their colourful clothes, Collen saw only evil in it – he likened the red to burning (hell) and the blue to coldness (death). The saint threw the holy water over the king and his courtiers, which caused them to disappear, leaving him alone on the hilltop. The manuscript 'Life of Saint Collen' by a Welsh saint of 650 AD documents this story.

At the top of the Tor is a tower, a 14th-century chapel dedicated to St. Michael. An earlier version built in the late 12th or early 13th century was destroyed in 1275 by an earthquake. Churches dedicated to St. Michael, the dragon slayer, were often built by Christians on old sacred mounds or sites.

There are many stories about a series of tunnels under the Tor. Does Gwyn ap Nudd still inhabit the Tor?

Many individuals have witnessed strange light phenomena on Glastonbury Tor or have felt disorientated and weightless. Local people sometimes feel compelled to climb to the top of the Tor, whereas other days they feel unable to go anywhere near it.

One of my personal experiences of the Tor was in 2000, when a friend and I climbed it at midnight on the winter solstice. Strangely enough, when we reached the summit we were the only ones there. There was a very powerful elemental quality on the Tor. We felt the presence of many magical beings and Archangel Michael was undoubtedly there. Glastonbury Tor is definitely a place of Faery visions and magic.

CONNECTING WITH SACRED-SITE FAERIES

Sacred sites are a wonderful place to visit particularly when you feel tired and unbalanced and you need to 'recharge your batteries'.

Go to whichever sacred site you feel drawn to — follow your intuition. It is not necessary to visit a famous ancient stone site such as Stonehenge. you can 'sense' and gain a great deal from a single standing stone.

Approach the sacred site slowly and with reverence. Keep an open heart and mind. Ask the sacred-site Faeries if you may be permitted to enter.

Go to whichever stone you feel drawn to. Stand or sit with your back against the stone making sure that you feel comfortable and relaxed. Close your eyes and connect with the energies.

Allow any tension to be released and transmitted by the earth. Then feel the power of the stone energising and revitalising your whole being.

Stay in the presence of the sacred-site Faeries for as long as you wish. As you open your eyes, notice you strong, calm and centred you are.

Thank the Faeries for sharing their power and wisdom with you and move slowly away from the ancient site.

A to Z of
MAGICAL
BEINGS

This section contains brief details of the main Faeries from all over the world. As you will see, they come in all shapes and sizes and there are bad Faeries as well as good ones!

A

ABATWA
Tiny, South African Faeries who live in anthills. Extremely shy, they only ever appear to young children and pregnant women. Apparently, if a woman sees one in the seventh month of her pregnancy she will give birth to a boy!

ABHAC
Abhac is derived from the word 'abha' meaning river. An Abhac is an Irish dwarf or water Faery and is cognate (related by blood; having a common ancestor) with the Welsh AFRANC.

ABUNDIA
Also known as Habundia, she is Queen of the Normandy Faeries or White Ladies. Reference is made to her in documents of the Middle Ages as a Faery Queen. Abundia is a Faery of great beauty. She has long dark hair and wears a circlet with a star on her forehead.

ACORN LADY
The Acorn Lady appears as a dwarf clad in peasant clothes. She abhors lazy humans and will pinch them! If you take an acorn from her tree she will punish you with cramps and bloating.

ADARO
The Adaro is a merman, half-human and half-fish, who comes from the Solomon Islands. Adaros live in the sun and travel to earth on rainbows; when on earth they travel on waterspouts. They are dangerous to humans as they shoot them with flying fish, causing unconsciousness, paralysis and even death.

AEDA
An Irish dwarf the size of a three-year-old child.

AELF
A Scandinavian elf whose name means 'shining spirit'.

AENGUS
One of the Irish Faeries of the TUATHA DÉ DANANN. He lives in a mound called Bruig na Boinne, the prehistoric site of Newgrange in Co. Meath, Ireland. A very handsome Faery with four birds that represent his kisses, hovering around his head.

AES SIDHE
Irish Faeries who live in the ancient hills and burial grounds. The name means 'People of the Hills'.

AFRANC
A Welsh water Faery with claws who is able to throw spears. Afranc is cognate (related by blood; having a common ancestor) with the Irish ABHAC.

AGUANE
An Aguane is a female Faery of Northern Italy and the Southern Slavonic and Austrian borders. She guards streams and mountains and her permission should be sought prior to bathing or she may wrap her hair around your feet and drown you or possibly eat you! These Faeries are shapeshifters, although usually they are beautiful with

long hair. They are dressed in fur and have the feet of goats or horses. They can also appear as old hags. Aguane are fond of small children who they carry on their backs.

AHL AL-TRAB
Tiny, mischievous Faeries of the Sahara desert.

ALP
A German Faery who likes to get into houses at night to play tricks and cause nightmares by sitting on your chest and pressing down hard.

ALVEN
Dutch water Faeries who live in ponds, lakes and rivers. Their main abode is the River Elbe. They cherish their flowers and will harm any human who tries to pick or harm their night wort, elf leaf or other sacred plants. They look almost transparent and are so light that they can travel through the air in water bubbles. Alven become visible if they wear the skins of otters.

ANKOU
A Breton Faery who comes to collect the souls of passed-over humans. Each village in Brittany has its own Ankou: the last man in the parish to die each year. He is the Grim Reaper who wears black hooded robes. No one has ever looked at his face and lived.

ANNWYN
The underworld where souls travel to after death.

ASHRAYS
Scottish water Faeries, both male and female, who are nocturnal. If exposed to sunlight they melt into a rainbow pool of water. They have pale ghost-like bodies.

ATUA
Polynesian Faeries who live in the trees.

AUKI
A Peruvian mountain Faery living in the Andes.

B

BAGAN
A Russian Faery who looks after livestock.

BALLYBOGS
Otherwise known as Bogles, Peat Faeries and Bog-a-boos, they dwell in and are the guardian spirits of peat bogs. Small, round, mud-covered creatures with spindly arms and legs they grunt and dribble instead of speaking.

BANNIK
A Russian house Faery.

BANSHEE
Otherwise known as the Bean Sidhe, or 'woman of the mound', she is much feared in Ireland. She has long, straggly hair, huge hollow eye sockets and fiery red eyes from continuous weeping. She wears a white shroud that gives her a ghost-like appearance and her piercing bone-chilling wail can be heard prior to a death.

BEAN FIONN
A white-robed Faery who lives beneath lakes and streams in Ireland and reaches up to drag children playing nearby under and drown them.

BEAN NIGHE
A type of Banshee found in the legends of Ireland, Scotland and Brittany. She washes the bloodstained shrouds of those who are about to die.

BEAN TIGHE
An Irish Faery home-keeper who watches over children and pets. If you leave these kindly elderly peasant women a bowl of cream they will finish your chores for you.

BEFANA
An Italian Faery who on the eve of 6th January places gifts in the stockings of good children and leaves pebbles for naughty children. Children leave her notes in the chimney.

BEFIND
An Irish Faery godmother who is present at a child's birth, together with two other Faeries.

BLANQUETTES
Small French Faeries who dress in white.

BOGEYMAN
A frightening, nasty Faery used to frighten the weak and threaten naughty children. He lives in the cupboard under the stairs.

BOGGART
A dark, hairy Faery with long, yellow teeth common in the north of England. Some say that his appearance is an omen of death, but others say that Boggarts are home Faeries that have turned evil and will wreck homes.

BOOBRIE
A Scottish Faery water bird, a foot (30 cm) high, with an enormous three-foot (1 m) bill. Boobries attack ships, transporting sheep and cattle, and lure their prey to the side of the ship by imitating the sound of their young.

BRODARICA VILA
Balkan water Faeries that live in streams, lakes or brooks and come out on moonlit nights to bathe their children.

BROWNIE
A house Faery who lives in a family and does odd jobs around the house in return for a bowl of milk and honey. Brownies live in attics, cellars and woodsheds or hollow trees and usually dress in ragged brown clothes but they may also wear green or blue suits and caps. They have

pointed ears and nimble fingers. When the cock crows, brownies go to bed.

BUCCA DHU
An evil Cornish Faery.

BUCCA GWIDDEN
A good Cornish water Faery.

BUG
An evil English Faery.

BWCA
Welsh Faeries, rather like brownies, who will perform tasks for you in return for a bowl of cream. If they are unfed, however, they can become destructive.

C

CAILLEAC BHUER
Otherwise known as the 'Blue Hag' this Scottish Faery lives on Ben Nevis. The Hebrides were formed from stones that fell from her basket. She wears blue-white tattered garments, her face is blue with cold and her hair as white as frost. The Blue Hag walks at night with her carrion crow on her left shoulder and carries a holly staff with the head of a carrion crow on the end. If she touches anyone with it they will die. At Beltane (1st May), she flings it under a holly tree as her power is gone. She returns at Samhain (1st November).

CALLICANTZAROI
Greek Faeries who are small and naked with horse's feet and wear red caps. They ride chickens, instead of horses. Almost blind, they love to gather at the Winter Solstice to celebrate the rebirth of the sun.

CEASG
A Scottish mermaid with the upper body of a woman and the tail of a salmon who lures men into the sea. However, if captured a Ceasg will grant three wishes.

CENTAURS
They have the upper bodies of men and the lower bodies of animals, usually horses, but sometimes donkeys or fish.

CERRIDWEN
A Welsh hag associated with the Underworld and famous for brewing a magic potion in her cauldron that contained all the wisdom of the ages.

CHANGELINGS
Faery babies that are substituted for human babies. They are usually ugly, deformed, weak or ailing and cry continuously. Unfortunately, in the past, any sick child was suspected of being a changeling and would be subjected to various tests. It might have been put out on a dunghill all day or placed on a shovel held over the fire saying:

'Burn, burn, burn

If of the devil, burn

But if of God and the saints

Be safe from harm'

CHIN-CHIN KOBAKAMA
Japanese home Faeries, elven-like in appearance, similar to the western BROWNIE. They pay particular attention to cleaning rugs and floors and can become a nuisance if the home is not kept clean.

CLURICHAUN
An Irish Faery who resembles his cousin the LEPRECHAUN. He is well-dressed in a green coat with large buttons and shoes with large metal buckles and a cocked hat. He likes to make shoes, drink and smoke tobacco. His purpose is to guard wine cellars and he will prevent casks from

leaking and wine from going bad if you show kindness to him. Otherwise he will wreak havoc.

COBLYNAU
Welsh mine Faeries, similar to the CORNISH KNOCKERS.

CORMORAN
A giant who built St. Michael's Mount in Cornwall and also the giant in the story Jack and the Beanstalk.

CORRIGANS
They guard sacred springs and fountains near stones in Brittany and Cornwall. Very common in the forest of Brocéliande, they appear as beautiful blonde females by night yet are repulsive hags by day.

COURIL
Small Breton Faeries that guard stone circles and standing stones. They are also found in Cornwall.

CRIONS
French Faeries that guard ancient standing stones. These small, dark creatures will force men to dance with them until they drop down dead with exhaustion.

CURUPIRA
A forest hobgoblin or wild man of Brazil who is said to have green teeth and feet and heels at the front of its feet to mislead trackers. He protects tortoises from hunters in the forests.

CYCLOPS
One-eyed man eating giants of classical Greek myth.

D

DAGDA
Chief god of the TUATHA DÉ DANANN and Faery King. His magical cauldron can restore life to the dead and his harp plays itself to change the seasons.

DAMES VERTES

Faeries of eastern France who live in the forest. These very tall, beautiful Faeries clad in green frequent caves, springs and waterfalls. They play tricks on travellers or may even lure young men to their deaths.

DEDUSKA

A Russian house Faery who appears as an old man covered in hair wearing a red shirt, cloak and belt. While everyone sleeps, he performs chores and protects the family, home and their livestock. Each property has its own Deduska and if a new home is built, certain rituals are performed to invite a Deduska in. When moving house, the family will ask their house Faery to accompany them.

DEVA

Nature spirits who appear as bright pulsating spheres of light. The word 'deva' comes from Persian and means 'shining one'.

DIANA

Queen of the Faeries in Roman folklore she is the goddess of the moon and hunt.

DJINN

Westerners are familiar with the Djinn, otherwise known as the Jinn or Genie on account of the Persian folktale 'Aladdin and the Magic Lamp'. They are the Arabian Faeries, referred to in the Koran, formed of smokeless fire, created thousand of years before Adam and Eve. Djinn have enormous powers of magic and can shapeshift. They live in lamps and bottles, from which they appear when summoned by their masters to do their bidding.

DOGIR

Water Faeries who live in the River Nile.

DRACS

French water Faeries who live under the River Seine and in the English Channel. Dracs like to mate with human men. They lure them by changing their natural state of floating purple blobs into beautiful woman. Alternatively, Dracs appear as a golden chalice and if a man reaches down to grab it they will drag him under the water.

DRAKES

English, German and Scandinavian fire Faeries who cannot be seen but are smell! The stench of rotten eggs betrays their presence. These house Faeries keep your firewood dry in return for living in your home.

DRYADS

Tree-dwelling spirits particularly fond of oak, willow, ash, thorn, rowan, elder and birch trees. They taught the Druids the secrets of tree magic.

DUENDES

Spanish house Faeries, male and female, who attach themselves to a family. They do not fear holy water and cannot be exorcised. Duendes are extremely house-proud and wish to get rid of the humans who make such a mess. They move and throw objects around, throw stones at the windows and pinch and poke humans with their long fingers in the night.

DUERGAR

Unpleasant dwarfs who like to play malicious tricks on travellers. They guard Faery paths, steer humans away from them and remove the signposts.

DWARF

Dwarfs live in the Scandinavian and German mountains and are male with short squat bodies, grey beards and wrinkles. They mature at three and are grey by the age of seven. They mine, guard precious stones and metals and must avoid sunlight, which turns them to stone.

DWERG

A Dutch dwarf.

E

ELF

Elves are known worldwide. In English folklore, elves are mostly trooping Faeries – they live in groups ruled by a King or a Queen. They dress mostly in green. In Scotland, elves are thought to be human-size. In Norse mythology, there are the white or light elves who are good and the black or dark elves who are evil.

Elves like to dance and play tricks. They are well-known for spinning cloth and making shoes.

ELLEFOLK

Danish Faeries that live on moorland marshes or next to rivers. Females are about 4 feet (1.2 m) tall with long, golden hair, hollow backs and cow's tails. Males are shorter and resemble old men. Ellefolk can see the future and are guardians of ancient secrets.

ELLYLLONS

They guard the domain of the 'Lady of the Lake' in Brocéliande, France and in Dosmary Pool, Cornwall, England.

ERDLUITLE

Faeries found in Northern Italy and Switzerland who live in mountains, caves or beneath standing stones. About 1–2 feet (30–60 cm) tall, with dark grey hair. They wear long cloaks to hide their duck feet. Usually friendly to humans, they increase the fertility of the land and protect animals. Erdluitle can influence all aspects of nature.

ERLKONIG

The Elf King appears in Germany and Denmark wearing a golden crown and beautiful clothes. He is an omen of death.

F

FACHAN

This Highland Faery has one eye, one ear, one arm, one leg, one toe and one finger that are all positioned on the middle of his hairy, feathered body. The Fachan wields a spiked club with which he attacks any humans who approach his mountain territory.

FAERY GODMOTHERS

They appear three days after the birth of a baby to bless it, foretell its future and give advice. Faery godmothers may also appear at weddings and at death. They love honey, almonds, bread and cake.

FATA

Generic Italian term for Faery.

FATES

The trio in classical mythology who determine the destiny of every human.

FAUN

Fauns are mischievous spirits of the woods that are the Roman equivalent of Greek satyrs (woodland spirits who look like handsome men with various animal features such as horse's tails, goat's legs and small horns on their foreheads). Fauns love to dance and play flutes.

FÉES

French Faeries, mostly female, who are usually small, young and beautiful but have a defect such as a tail. A few are old hags. They can turn themselves into whatever they want, such as stones or trees, or even become invisible. Fées live in mounds, dolmens, caves, woods and forests. They are ruled by Queen Abundia.

FION

Tiny Breton Faeries.

FIRE DRAKES

Dragon-like creatures with long necks, bat wings and enormous jaws recorded in Celtic and Germanic folklore. They are cunning, breathe fire and guard treasure.

FOLLETTI

Italian Faeries who look like children and have their feet on backwards or they may appear as butterflies. Folletti are the offspring of FAUNS or SILVANI. Generally they are kind to humans, but some can be wicked and every Italian district has a formula for exorcising them.

FORMORIANS

Sea monsters from Ireland driven into the sea by the TUATHA DÉ DANANN. They have grotesque bodies made up from the leftover parts of animals.

FOSSEGRIM

Norwegian water Faeries that guard waterfalls and Fjords. They have beautiful singing voices and are expert harpists.

FYLGJA

An Icelandic protective spirit that any child born with a caul over its head will be accompanied by throughout life. (A caul is the membrane in the womb, a part of which sometimes covers a baby's head when it is born.) A Fylgja can only be seen by a human prior to death.

G

GANS

Apache Faeries who guard the mountains of south-western North America. They bring good luck and drive away evil spirits.

GEANCANACH

Small house Faeries of Northern Ireland.

GHILLIE DHU

A Scottish Faery who protects trees, especially birch trees, from humans. Ghillie Dhu literally means 'dark shoe'.

GIANES

Italian elves who spend their time spinning and even carry small spinning wheels in their pockets. About 5 feet (1.5 m) tall with long hair and steel fingernails, Gianes wear furs and hats made of animal skins. They are expert diviners.

GIANTS

Giants look like humans but are much larger. They are found all over the world and legends say that giants built the ancient monuments.

GLAISTIG

A Scottish Faery, small with yellow hair down to her feet, but with the half-body of a goat. The Glaistig is a human woman under Faery enchantment. She preys on human males who she drowns or sucks their blood.

GNOME

An elemental Faery of the earth who reaches maturity at the age of one hundred and lives for about one thousand years. Gnomes are about 12 inches (30 cm) tall and wear pointed red hats. Their faces are kind and cheerful.

Gnomes live under oak trees in ancient forests, although many ceramic and plastic gnomes grace our gardens.

GOBLIN

The word 'goblin' may be derived from the Greek word 'kobaloi' meaning evil spirits. It is a generic term for the more unpleasant, ugly, malicious Faeries.

GORGONS

Mermaids in Greek folklore who are half-woman and half-fish.

GREEN MAN

A very ancient figure depicted in stonework and timber carvings, the Green Man is known worldwide as a vegetation God. His head is seen covered with leaves. The King of Green Men is said to live in the New Forest, Hampshire, England.

GREMLINS

Gremlins range in size from tiny to almost human-sized. They are strong, hairy all over, green, blue or grey with wide grins. Gremlins wreak havoc with machinery, During World War II pilots reported seeing hairy creatures riding on their aircraft!

GRIGS

Tiny British Faeries about the size of a grasshopper. They are always happy, hence the expression 'as happy as a grig'.

GROGOCH

An Irish house Faery.

GRUAGACH

A female Scottish Faery who protects and looks after cattle. Many rural cattleherders leave milk for her in a hollow stone known as a Gruagach's stone.

GWRAGEDD ANNWYN

Very beautiful blonde water Faeries living beneath the lakes in the Black Mountains of Wales. They love children and help mothers and the poor.

GWYLLIONS

Welsh mountain Faeries who care for herds of goats. They are very ugly and can shapeshift into goats. They dislike humans intensely and lead them off paths into swamps.

GWYN AP NUDD

Welsh King of the Underworld.

H

HAMADRYADS

Tree spirits who are female to the waist, with their lower parts forming the trunk and roots of the tree. When the tree dies so does the Hamadryad.

HEINZEMANNCHEN

A small dwarf found in German folklore. Provided they are fed once a week they will do most of the housework.

HOBGOBLIN

Commonly found in England, they are hairy, good-natured house Faeries about 1–2 feet (30–60 cm) tall. They can turn into troublesome BOGGARTS if offended. Hobgoblins love to sit around a warm fire.

HOLDA FRAU

According to German folklore this beautiful Faery makes the snow fall as she shakes out her bed of feathers in the sky.

HULDRE

Scandinavian elves whose name means 'Hidden Folk'. They can give humans a deformity by licking them with their dark brown tongues.

HYLDERMODER

Guardian spirit of the sacred elder tree. She is protective and kindly unless humans damage an elder tree.

I

IELES

Found in Romania and Eastern Europe, Ieles look like huge cats that walk on two legs. They wait at crossroads for human victims and suck their blood. Ieles love dancing and music and force humans to join in with them. If you ever come across one, go to the middle of the crossroads since Ieles lose their power there.

ILLES

Icelandic trolls who live underground and only come out after sunset. They are hairy, dark and naked in their natural state, but they can shapeshift into beautiful women to attract men who will then pine away and die. Illes can make a person sick just by touching them.

IMP

A wicked Faery or a small demon. The Old English word 'impe' means 'young shoot'. Therefore, an imp is a 'young shoot' of his father, the Devil.

INCUBIS

An evil male spirit who sexually assaults a woman in her sleep. ('cuba'=to lie, 'in'=upon). If she becomes pregnant she gives birth to a wizard.

J

JACK FROST

The English Faery who brings the winter frosts and nips noses, toes and fingers.

JACK-A-LANTERN

This Faery is similar to a WILL-O'-THE-WISP. It lives in bogs and marshes and tricks humans, leading them into the bogs or marshlands, where they are drowned.

JENDZYNA

An evil, ugly Polish spirit of the forest that steals children and inflicts harm on adults.

JIMANINOS

Winged Faeries of Mexico and America who look like small podgy children. Some believe they are the souls of dead children.

JOULUPUKKI

This Finnish Faery appears in

the form of a goat and at Christmas leaves presents in children's stockings hung upon the hearth or in their shoes placed at the door.

K

KACHINAS

Spirits, thought to be the souls of good people, summoned by the Hopi and Pueblo Indians of North America. The Kachina Dancers wear masks representative of the spirits to enlist their help – for instance in rainmaking.

KAPPA

Japanese water spirits with green skin, webbed and clawed hands, tortoiseshells on their backs and small depressions on their heads filled with water. Kappas can't survive very long out of water. They travel around on cucumbers and are very dangerous, as they love human flesh!

KELPIES

Scottish cannibalistic water Faeries with shapeshifting powers. At one time they lived under Loch Ness. They appear as friendly seahorses but once mounted by a human they carry them off and eat them.

KILLMOULIS

An ugly Scottish brownie who, since he has no mouth, eats by stuffing food up his enormous nose.

KNOCKERS

Also known as Knackers they are one of the most well-known Faeries of Cornwall. They are dwarf-like and live in tin mines and caves. Knockers in Wales are called COBLYNAUS. They are small and ugly with hook noses and mouths like large slits. Their name is derived from the knocking sound they make when directing miners to a good seam in return for a morsel of pastry. Sometimes they play games with the miners, who are very respectful to them. Cornish miners will not enter a mine if they hear frantic knocking and they will never upset Knockers by swearing or whistling.

KOBOLD

A house or mine Faery found in Germany particularly but also in Austria, Switzerland and Scandinavia. They are dwarf-like with dark-green or dark-grey skin, hairy tails and wear pointed shoes and hats. A Kobold will work around the house in return for scraps of food. However, if they are ignored, they will turn malicious and will engage in poltergeist activity. They are also found in mines where cobalt is dug.

KORREDS / KORRS

The Faery guardians of the dolmens and stone circles of Brittany. Some claim it was the Korreds who erected the megalithic monuments. Korrs are incredibly strong with enormous heads and hairy bodies. They have cloven feet, cat's claws, spindly arms and legs, rough voices and always carry a pair of scissors in a leather purse. Despite their appearance, they are not malicious towards humans unless they desecrate the stones. Korreds will sharpen a knife, or any other sharp tool,if you leave it by the stones overnight.

KRACKEN

A Scandinavian sea monster so enormous it can swallow a boat.

L

LAMIA

A seductive spirit who appears as an exquisitely beautiful woman but can change into a serpent.

LAR

A protective spirit of ancient Rome. For instance, the Lar Familaris protected the home, the Lares Compitales guarded boundaries, the Lares Praestites protected citizens and the Lares Semitales protected paths.

LEANAN SIDHE

A beautiful Faery from Ireland, Scotland or the Isle of Man who seeks a human partner. She sucks the life out of her mortal partner. The Isle of Man 'Lhiannan Shee' is a bloodsucker.

LEPRECHAUN

A well-known, male Irish Faery, who is the cobbler for the Faery gentry (although he only works on one shoe, never a pair) and guards a pot of gold. Leprechauns wear green clothes with silver buttons, leather aprons, three-cornered hats and silver-buckled shoes. They love whisky, tobacco, music, dancing and foxhunting. Leprechauns are very fond of riddles and word games. It is said that if you capture a Leprechaun he will give you his crock of gold and three wishes. But the Leprechaun will outwit you and trick you.

LESHIE

Russian Faeries who are the offspring of human women and demons. Active from spring to autumn, they are the guardians of the forest. A Leshie can shapeshift, appearing as a tree or a blade of grass. They are green or blue with bark-like skin and the horns and feet of a goat. Leshiye will trick travellers by removing signposts and lure women into the forest to molest them. For protection wear your shoes on the wrong feet or your clothes back to front.

LITTLE SPIRITS
Small Faeries, about 1 1/2 inches (4 cm) high, who guard the territory of the native America Sioux indians.

LOB
A Welsh goblin that looks like a rain cloud. He stays alive by feeding off energies from arguments and fights.

LORELEI
A beautiful German water Faery dwelling in the River Rhine who sings to lure sailors onto the rocks.

LUDKI
Dwarfs found in Slavonic folklore who love music and singing. In return for millet they will perform chores around the house. Ludki also live in mountains and forests. They are mortal, (unlike other Faeries), and when they die their ashes are put into pots and buried in the earth.

LUTINS
Found in France, especially Brittany and Normandy, Lutins are expert shapeshifters. They live in caves, near water or standing stones, or even in human homes, although they never stay in one place for long. If they do act as house Faeries and are offended they become malicious.

M

MAB
Queen of the Welsh Faeries.

MANANNAN
The Isle of Man is named after this Faery. Once a Celtic sea-god he looks like a three-legged wheel.

MANNIKIN
A German term for elves.

MAZIKEEN
Winged Faeries found in Jewish folklore. They were the offspring of Adam and Eve, created after they were banished from the Garden of Eden. Mazikeen can shapeshift, make themselves invisible, perform magic and see the future.

MENAHUNE
Well-known Hawaiian Faeries living in the forests, they are 6–24 inches (15–60 cm) tall, with long black hair and pointed ears. Menahune only come out at night when they love to dance and sing and dive into the sea. They can be tricksters and as they are unpredictable the islanders avoid them. Manahune are thought to guard hidden treasure.

MERMAIDS
Mermaids have the upper bodies of beautiful women and the lower bodies of fish. They live in sunken wrecks and love to sit on rocks singing and combing their hair. Mermaids do not have souls but can gain one if they marry a human. They are usually friendly and sailors have recorded many instances of mermaids steering their ships to safety. Mermen, however, can be malicious and cause storms.

MONACHICCHIO
A Faery native to Calabria in the southernmost region of the Italy who dresses like a monk. He wears an enormous red hood, twice the size of his body, and guards underground treasure. If you steal his hood he will tell you where the treasure is, for without his hood he will die.

MORGENS
Very beautiful, Breton water Faeries who are eternally young. The Morgen only ventures out at night to comb her hair in the moonlight, enticing sailors to her with her beautiful voice. If a sailor touches her he will die.

MOSS PEOPLE
German Faeries, both male and female, who have huge butterfly wings. Their purpose is to spin the moss for the forests and they are covered in moss to blend in with the trees. They abhor humans who damage the forests, but will help humans with their healing power and knowledge of plants.

MURYANS
Tiny Cornish Faeries the size of ants – the Cornish word 'murrain' means 'ant'. In Cornwall it is believed to be unlucky to kill ants, since they think that ants may be the final forms of small Faeries.

N

NAGAS
Indian NYMPHS who protect springs, wells, streams, waterfalls, lakes and rivers. They can appear as beautiful women or as serpents.

NAIADS
Water NYMPHS in Greek mythology.

NECK
A Scandinavian shapeshifting water Faery who is an expert harpist. He is handsome, with golden hair, but he demands a human sacrifice every year.

NEPTUNES
Small, mischievous, French water Faeries.

NEREIDES
Sea NYMPHS most often seen in the Aegean Sea. They are beautiful and graceful with shell headdresses. The Nereides love to sing. They are jealous of human mothers and try to harm their children or steal them. An offering of milk and honey may distract them.

NICKEL

German name for a Goblin, or a mischievous water or mine Faery.

NIS

A Scandinavian house Faery about 6 inches (15 cm) high. He has the face of an old man and wears a pointed red cap.

NISKEN

German house Faeries.

NIXEN

German water Faeries who wear red caps. Child Nixens are called URCHINS. A Nix may replace a human being with a changeling. They are expert fiddlers but humans should not play the 'Elf King's Tune' or they will not be able to stop until the strings are cut or until they can play it backwards. A Nixie is a female German water Faery. She loves to seduce handsome young men and lure them into the water, never to be seen again.

NORGGEN

These male Faeries, found in Northern Italy, are said to be amongst the oldest in existence. They are forest Faeries clad in coats covered in moss, and three-cornered hats. Norggen steal from humans, although they are usually friendly except when angered.

NYMPH

A classification applied to female nature spirits and Faeries. They include water nymphs such as NAIADS, sea-nymphs such as NEREIDES and tree-nymphs such as DRYADS. They are all very beautiful and seductive.

O

OAF

A CHANGELING (Faery child) left in place of a human baby who is deformed or stupid.

OAK MEN

The guardians of oak trees who become angry if the trees are harmed.

OGRE

A male or female, large, deformed, ugly Faery, who is hairy, fearless and often harmful towards humans.

P

PAN

Son of Hermes, Pan is the most powerful nature spirit. He has hairy lower limbs, the feet of a goat and wears a spotted fawn skin. Pan is famous for playing his pipes.

PERI

Persian good Faeries formed from fire, Peries fight with the DEEVS, the evil Faeries. At one time the Peries were responsible for bad weather, poor harvests and comets but they were transformed into beautiful Faeries who guide souls to paradise.

PHOOKA

An Irish shapeshifting goblin, who may take the form of a goat, dog, horse, bull or eagle. To 'play the phooka' means 'to play the devil'. In Ireland Halloween is known as 'Phooka Night'.
The Phooka loves to taunt travellers – in horse form he offers them a ride, gallops off wildly and then drops them in a ditch. Their favourite food is potatoes, which they dig from fields at nighttime.

PILLYWIGGIN

A very small winged Faery who lives amongst the wild flowers.

PISKIES

Cornish pixies, who many Cornish people believe are the souls of prehistoric dwellers in Britain. They think that they will decrease in size until they vanish completely. Piskies are described as little old men with bright eyes, green stockings and polished shoes.

PIXIES

Small green Faeries who live in the West Country, especially in Dartmoor. They have pointed ears and noses and arched eyebrows and wear foxglove or toadstool caps. They love to dance and the tinkling of their bells can often be heard. Pixies are full of mischief and steal wild ponies at night and knot their manes. They also lead travellers off the path – known as being 'pixie-led'. To find your way turn your clothes inside out.

POLEVIK

Faeries of the Russian fields (especially cornfields) who grow to the size of the crops. After the harvest they lay claim to all the grain that is left in the fields. Polish farmers often leave grain out for them.

PORTUNES

Britain's oldest recorded Faeries. They look like small, wrinkled old men and love practical jokes. Portunes do chores in return for milk.

PUCK

An English Faery of the woods who appears in Shakespeare's 'A Midsummer Night's Dream'. Puck has the head of a young man with horns on his head and the body of a goat. He is the son of a Faery father and a mortal mother. He is very mischievous and plays pranks such as shapeshifting into a horse.

PYRENEES

Faeries who guard the ancient standing stones of Cornwall.

R

RED CAP

A malevolent Scottish Faery found in old castle ruins and towers. A Red Cap looks old with a leathery body, long grey hair and a beard. He has piercing red eyes, protruding teeth and long, sharp fingernails. He wears a red cap, which he dyes with the blood of his victims. Once the blood is dry he seeks a new victim.

RUSALKI

Rusalkis are beautiful Russian water Faeries with long, loose, green or blonde hair. They dress in green leaves and take care to keep their hair moist, for if it dries out they will die.

Rusalkis bathe and play in the water and comb their hair in the moonlight. Men need to take care, for the Rusalkis lure men to them with their songs then destroy them by drowning or tickling!

S

SALAMANDERS

Elemental Faeries of the fire.

SANDMAN

A Faery found in Europe and North American who gives children pleasant dreams by sprinkling their eyes with magical sand.

SATYRS

Ancient Greek forest spirits who accompany PAN and Dionysus and chase NYMPHS.

SEELIE COURT

The Seelie Court are the good Faery forms of Scottish folklore as opposed to the UNSEELIE COURT that is composed of bad Faeries. They are full of compassion for humans.

SELKIES

Water Faeries native to Scotland and the Orkney Islands, who appear as seals in the sea but, on coming ashore, can shed their sealskins. They come ashore to dance but, if disturbed, they will put on their sealskins and retreat to the safety of the sea. A man can force a Selkie to marry him if he can steal her seal skin, but she will never be happy. Male Selkies sometime cause storms to overturn the boats of seal hunters.

SILVANI

Italian wood Faeries –half-man and half-goat. They wear animal furs and protect trees and wildlife. Silvani adore the colour red.

SIRENS

Greek sea NYMPHS who sing seductive songs of enchantment to lure men to their deaths.

SPRIGGANS

Evil Faeries living in Cornwall who are small and round but are capable of inflating themselves until they are the size of giants. They are very destructive, blight crops, steal and substitute human babies for CHANGELING.

SUCCUBUS

A female spirit who sexually assaults a man in his sleep to conceive a child of the devil.

SYLPH

An air elemental whose name means 'butterfly'. Sylphs are small, winged creatures who are almost transparent.

T

TENGU

Japanese nature spirits who are part of the old Shinto religion. They have great magical powers and can shapeshift.

THUSSERS

Norwegian Faeries who live in mounds near the fjords.

TITANIA

The 'Queen of the Faeries' in Shakespeare's 'A Midsummer Night's Dream'.

TOOTH FAERY

The tooth Faery comes when a child has lost a milk tooth. Commonly, she is very small, and she comes in the middle of the night. The child leaves the tooth under the pillow so that the tooth can take it during her visit. Once she has taken the tooth, she leaves some money under the pillow. The teeth are then taken to her tower and used for her purposes.

TROLL

Trolls are large, hairy, ugly creatures who dislike humans. They emerge at night, since sunlight will turn them into stone. Trolls are well-known as the guardians of bridges – as in the folktale of Aarne-Thompson 'The Three Billy Goats Gruff'. They throw rocks at other creatures and laugh for no reason, because they are incredibly stupid.

TUATHA DÉ DANANN

These legendary Gods of Ireland were literally the 'People of the Goddess Danu'. These tall Faery creatures were eventually defeated by the Milesian Celts and retreated into the mounds where they can still be found.

TWLWYTH TEG

Small Faeries known as the 'Fair Family' or 'Mother's Blessing' that live on Faery islands off the Welsh coast that are connected to the mainland by tunnels. They are ruled by GWYN AP NUDD, God of the Dead.

U

UNDINES
Ancient Greek sea Faeries found in the Aegean Sea, who look like seahorses with human faces.

UNICORN
A white horse with a single horn in the centre of its forehead that dwells in Faeryland. It is a symbol of purity.

UNSEELIE COURT
The Unseelie Court is composed of malevolent Scottish Faeries. They are evil and are believed to be the souls of the damned.

URCHIN
Child of a NIXIE.

V

VAMPIRES
Faeries who suck the blood of humans to drain the life force from them.

VASILY
Russian Faeries who love and care for horses. They are small with hoofs and horse ears and live in stables.

VILY
Slavonic female Faeries mentioned in ancient Russian writings. The name means 'whirlwind' and refers to their appearance during storms. They are beautiful Faeries who wear white dresses or green leaves. Their long, curly auburn hair is the source of their strength. They live in the forests, clouds, stars, mountains or in the water. Their beauty and singing has entranced many a man.

VODIANOI
Russian water Faeries who are the male counterparts of the RUSALKI.

W

WATER LEAPERS
Welsh Faeries that bounce along the surface of the sea and prey on fisherman who they lure onto the rocks.

WELL GUARDIANS
Spirits who guard wells who must be rewarded with offerings of coins or pins if your wish is to be granted.

WICHTLEIN
Wichtlein are Faeries from Southern Germany who haunt mines and whose appearance is that of old men with long beards.

WICHTLN
German house Faeries who are small and dress in brown fur coats. They are extremely industrious, but, if they are not showered with gifts, Wichtln are very mischievous.

WILL-O'-THE-WISP
The Will-O'-The-Wisp is a strange flickering light that appears low to the ground near marshes. These strong lights can lead unwary travellers to their doom.

Y

YAKKUS
North American Faeries capable of shapeshifting.

YAKSHAS
Himalayan Faeries who guard treasure.

YETI
An enormous hairy creature who looks like a huge gorilla and is found in the remote areas of North America and East Asia.

Z

ZEPHYRS
Guardians of the winds.

ZIPS
Tiny male Faeries who wear little helmets and carry small spears. They live in Mexico and Central America and protect deer and stags.

ZWERGE
A German dwarf who lives underground surrounded by treasure. Zwergen can become invisible and can pass through rocks just as easily as a fish swims through water.

PROTECTION
FROM FAERIES

When I first started writing this book I imagined that most Faeries were gentle, beautiful, ethereal beings. As you can see from this A–Z of Magical Beings, Faeries often play tricks or can even be dangerous! Here are a few ways to protect you from Faery mischief:

· Faeries are petrified of iron. Keep a nail in your pocket and put one under your pillow at night. Or even hang a horseshoe on your door

· If you are being pixie-led turn your clothes inside out

· Throw a glove into a Faery ring if someone is trapped inside

· Keep a bible in the home

· Carry a holed stone

· Hang up a rowan cross tied with red thread

· Grow a mulberry tree in your garden

· Carry oatmeal in your pocket

· Scatter flax on the floor

· Carry some St. John's Wort

· Wear a daisy chain

· Leave the Faeries an offering such as milk and honey.

INDEX

USEFUL ADDRESSES

Denise Whichello Brown

MWB Business Exchange,
Hinton Road,
Bournemouth.
BH1 2EF
Tel: +44 (0)1202 708887
www.angel-therapy.com
info@angel-therapy.com
For details on angel and
Faery workshops by Denise
Whichello Brown.

Denise Brown Essential Oils

MWB Business Exchange,
Hinton Road,
Bournemouth.
BH1 2EF
Tel: +44 (0)1202 708887

www.denisebrown.co.uk

info@denisebrown.co.uk

A wide selection of high quality
pure unadulterated essential
oils, base oils, creams and
lotions, Faery sprays, relaxation
music etc. is available from
Denise Brown International
Mail Order.

Sue Harrington

P.O. Box 2083,
Shoreham-By-Sea.
BN43 5XZ
Tel: +44 (0)1273 464670
Doll Maker – ¹⁄₁₂th scale
porcelain Faery dolls including
viscose hair
www.sueharrington.net
Where you can see work by
Faery artists Jo Harrington and
Robyn Southee.

ACKNOWLEDGEMENTS

Thank you as always to my dear husband Garry.

Thanks also to my fellow travellers Julie, Colin and Garry and my Faery friend Jo.

PICTURE CREDITS

All fairy illustrations and line drawings by David Ashby
Illustration p14 by Chlóe Leaper
Photographs pp23, 25, 30t, 60, 88, 90, 93 by Denise Whichello Brown
Photograph p95 by Sarah King
Images pp 12, 18, 19, 29, 30b, 32, 57-59, 62, 64t, 68, 70, 89, 99, 102, 104, 107
© Getty Images
Images pp 38r, 40, 43, 45, 46, 49, 50
© Stockbyte
(b = bottom, r = right, t = top)